The Best Study Series for

GED

Social Studies

2nd Edition

Lynn Elizabeth Marlowe, M.A.

Research & Education Association
Visit our website at
www.rea.com

Research & Education Association
61 Ethel Road West
Piscataway, New Jersey 08854
E-mail: info@rea.com

3 3113 02330 7079

The Best Study Series for
GED SOCIAL STUDIES

Printed in the United States of America

Library of Congress Control Number 2005929496

International Standard Book Number 0-7386-0127-6

TABLE OF CONTENTS

Introduction

ABOUT THIS BOOK

Congratulations. You've taken an important step toward successfully earning your GED. This book is designed to help you take and pass the *Social Studies Test* of the GED. Perhaps you've decided to focus your study time on the single subject that's most difficult for you, or you may have already taken the GED and did not pass completely, and you've chosen REA's single-subject guides for targeted review. Whichever applies to your individual situation, you've made a great choice.

You will begin your prep for the GED *Social Studies Test* by learning what's expected of you on this exam. You will learn what topics are covered, how many questions to expect, and how much time you'll have to answer them. You will then move on to the subject review, where the subject matter will be discussed in much greater detail. The subject review in this book covers everything you'll need to know to pass the *Social Studies Test*. Be sure to complete the drills in each section, since they will be a great help in keeping on top of your progress. If you find that you are struggling with the drill questions in a given section, it may be a good idea to read that section again.

The formula for success on the GED is very simple: the more you study, the more likely you are to pass the exam. Know the material covered here, and you will be calm and confident on exam day.

ABOUT THE GED PROGRAM

For more than 60 years, the GED Examination has been administered by the GED Testing Service of the American Council on Education (ACE). The GED exam offers anyone who did not complete high school the opportunity to earn a High School Equivalency Certificate. With that certificate come many new opportunities for a better career or higher education.

The GED may be a step on your journey to a college degree, since almost one out of every twenty first-year college students has a GED. Or a GED may be your ticket to a better job and into a career with a bright future and room to grow. Whatever your academic or professional goals are, success on the GED is a great place to begin.

The GED exam is available in all 50 states and Canada. There are over 3,400 testing centers in North America, and another 2,800 testing centers worldwide, so you should have no problem finding a GED testing center near you.

For more information on the GED program, to find an administration schedule, or to find a testing center near you, start by contacting your local high school or adult education center. Or, you can contact the American Council on Education, which administers the GED, at:

GED – General Educational Development
American Council on Education
One Dupont Circle NW, Suite 250
Washington, DC 20036-1163

To contact the GED administrators by phone, call: (202) 939-9300 or (800) 626-9433 (Toll Free)

You can also e-mail them at comments@ace.nehu.edu, or visit them on the Web at *www.gedtest.org*.

Alternate-Language GED Tests

If English is not your first language, you may be able to take the GED exam in Spanish or French. Contact the GED administrators for more information.

Accommodations for Test Takers with Disabilities

If you have special needs because of a physical or learning disability, accommodations are available for you. Some examples of qualifying disabilities are blindness, deafness, dyslexia, dyscalculia, and attention-deficit/hyperactivity disorder. A complete list of qualifying disabilities is available from the GED test administrators. The proper accommodations can make a great deal of difference for those entitled to them, so be sure that you are taking the GED exam that's right for you.

If you believe that you have a qualifying disability but you do not have complete documentation, contact the National Rehabilitation Information Center (NARIC) at (800) 346-2742.

ABOUT THE GED EXAM

The GED exam consists of five separate subject tests. The breakdown is outlined in the chart below.

The entire exam is 7 hours and 30 minutes long. That sounds like a lot to cover! But don't worry. Each topic is treated individually. If you pass all five topics in one sitting, you've earned your GED. If you don't, you only have to take the section or sections that you did not pass.

An overview of the GED Tests

Test Area	Number of Questions	Time For Test	Test Format
Language Arts, Writing, Part I	50 questions	75 minutes	Organization (15%)
			Sentence Structure (30%)
			Usage (30%)
			Mechanics (25%)
Language Arts, Writing, Part II	1 essay	45 minutes	Written essay on assigned topic
Language Arts, Reading	40 questions	65 minutes	Literary Text (75%)
			Non-Literary Text (25%)
Mathematics	50 questions	90 minutes	Number operations and number sense (20%–30%)
			Measurement and geometry (20%–30%)
			Data analysis, statistics, and probability (20%–30%)
			Algebra, functions, and patterns (20%–30%)
Social Studies	50 questions	70 minutes	History (40%)
			Geography (15%)
			Civics/Government (25%)
			Economics (20%)
Science	50 questions	80 minutes	Physical Science (35%)
			Life Science (45%)
			Earth and Space Science (20%)

ABOUT THE SOCIAL STUDIES TEST

The *Social Studies Test* presents 50 multiple-choice questions from the content areas detailed below:

- History (United States or Canada, 25%; World, 15%)

- Geography (15%)

- Civics and Government (25%)

- Economics (20%)

(Note: There are different U.S. and Canadian versions of the *Social Studies Test*. This book prepares you for the U.S. edition.)

Most of the test questions are based on written and visual texts drawn from a variety of sources, including academic and workplace texts, along with primary and secondary sources. The information provided may take the form of one or more paragraphs of text, a chart, table, graph, map, photograph, cartoon, or figure. In every case, to answer the questions in the Social Studies Test, you must understand, apply, analyze, or evaluate the information provided.

WHEN SHOULD I START STUDYING?

If you're wondering when to start studying, the short answer is *now*. You may have a few days, a few weeks, or a few months to prepare for the particular administration of the GED that you're going to take. But in any case, the more time you spend studying for the GED, the better.

BEFORE THE TEST

At some point, you've studied all you can and test day is only one good night's sleep away. Be sure to go to bed early on the night before test day, and get as much rest as you can. Eat a good breakfast. Dress in layers that can be added or removed so you'll be comfortable if the testing center is warmer or cooler than you like. Plan to arrive at the test center at least 20 minutes early so that traffic or other transportation issues don't prevent you from getting to the test center on time. If you're not sure where the test center is, be sure to make the trip at least once before test day. On the morning of test day, your only job is to let nothing—not hunger, not temperature, not traffic—distract you from your main goal: success on the GED. Use the test-day checklist at the back of this book to make sure you've covered all the bases.

What to Bring with You
- Your admission ticket, if you need one
- An official photo ID
- Some sharpened No. 2 pencils (with erasers) and a blue or black ink pen
- A watch, if you have one.

The following items will *not* be allowed in the testing area, so if you choose to bring them, know that you will have to store them during the test:
- Purses and tote bags
- Electronic devices, including MP3 players, video games, pagers, cell phones, CD players, etc.
- Food
- Books and notebooks
- Other non-essential items

Remember that by the time you reach test day, you will have put in your study time, taken your practice exams, and learned the test format. You will be calm and confident, knowing that you're ready for the GED.

TOP TEST TIPS WHEN TAKING THE GED

While you're taking the GED, here are some important test strategies:

• Read all the directions carefully so that you understand what's expected of you. If you have questions, ask the GED examiner.

• Answer every question. There's no wrong-answer penalty on the GED, so if you don't know, *guess*. If you leave a question blank, you're guaranteed to get zero points. If you have to guess, you have a 20% chance of getting the question right.

• Smart guesses are better than random guesses. If you have five possible answers, and you have no idea which is correct, that's a random guess. If you have five possible answers

and you've eliminated three that are definitely wrong, that's a Smart Guess. You now have a 50% chance of getting the question right.

• Keep an eye on your time. Don't spend too much time on any one question. Choose your best answer, and move on. Come back to troublesome questions later, if there's time.

AFTER THE TEST

When you've completed your GED exam, you've reached the end of one journey and the beginning of another. You gave your best effort and it's a great feeling. Hopefully you've passed all five tests and you can look forward to a new world of opportunity. If you don't pass all five tests, you can focus your study time on only those areas that still need work. But remember, success begins with a goal, and whether you pass on your first try or not, your journey is well under way. Go home, relax, and take a well-deserved rest. You've earned it.

ABOUT RESEARCH & EDUCATION ASSOCIATION

Founded in 1959, Research & Education Association is dedicated to publishing the finest and most effective educational materials—including software, study guides, and test preps—for students in middle school, high school, college, graduate school, and beyond.

REA's Test Preparation series includes books and software for all academic levels in almost all disciplines. Research & Education Association publishes test preps for students who have not yet entered high school, as well as high school students preparing to enter college. Students from countries around the world seeking to attend college in the United States will find the assistance they need in REA's publications. For college students seeking advanced degrees, REA publishes test preps for many major graduate school admission examinations in a wide variety of disciplines, including engineering, law, and medicine. Students at every level, in every field, with every ambition can find what they are looking for among REA's publications.

REA's practice tests are always based upon the most recently administered exams, and include every type of question that you can expect on the actual exams.

REA's publications and educational materials are highly regarded and continually receive an unprecedented amount of praise from professionals, instructors, librarians, parents, and students. Our authors are as diverse as the fields represented in the books we publish. They are well-known in their respective disciplines and serve on the faculties of prestigious high schools, colleges, and universities throughout the United States and Canada.

We invite you to visit us at *www.rea.com* to find out how "REA is making the world smarter."

ACKNOWLEDGMENTS

Special recognition is extended to the following persons:

Larry Kling, Vice President, Editorial, for his overall direction.

Pam Weston, Vice President, Publishing, for setting the quality standards for production integrity and managing the publication to completion.

Stacey Farkas, Senior Editor, for project management.

John Paul Cording, Vice President, Technology, for his editorial contributions.

Christine Saul, Senior Graphic Artist, for designing our cover.

Jeff LoBalbo, Senior Graphic Artist, for post-production file mapping.

Network Typesetting, Inc., for typesetting the manuscript.

Social Studies

Pre-Test

SOCIAL STUDIES

PRE-TEST

> **DIRECTIONS:** Read each of the passages below and then answer the questions pertaining to them. Choose the <u>single best answer</u> to each question.

Questions 1–3 are based on the following passage.

The President of the United States is head of the executive branch. Any person running for President has to be at least thirty-five years old and be a natural born citizen of the United States. He or she must have resided in the country for fourteen years prior to being elected.

1. The President is head of which branch of the government?

   (1) Legislative.

   (2) Executive.

   (3) Judicial.

2. Which of the following statements is a fact?

   (1) Being President of the United States is the toughest job in the country.

   (2) The President does not have to live in the United States before being elected.

   (3) The President is the head of the executive branch.

3. A candidate for the presidency must be at least

   (1) 35 years old.

   (2) 21 years old.

   (3) '28 years old.

Questions 4–6 are based on the following passage.

Gold was discovered at Sutter's Mill, near Sacramento, California, in 1848. The next year gold-seekers from the eastern United States and many foreign countries went to California seeking gold. The population of California quickly grew from 14,000 to 100,000. Many of the gold-seekers proved to be rough characters and California became a wild and lawless place.

4. Where was gold discovered in 1848?

   (1) Milltown, California.

   (2) Los Angeles, California.

   (3) Sutter's Mill, California.

5. Why did the population of California grow so fast after 1848?

    (1) People went there seeking gold.

    (2) People wanted to live in a wild place.

    (3) The weather was good.

6. Which statement is a fact?

    (1) People love finding gold.

    (2) Gold was discovered in California in 1848.

    (3) It was scary to live in California during the 1800s.

Questions 7 and 8 are based on the following graph.

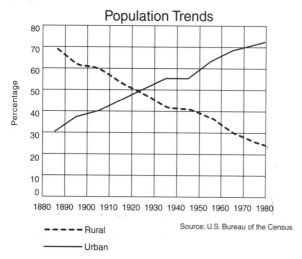

Population Trends

Source: U.S. Bureau of the Census

- - - - - Rural

————— Urban

7. In 1980

    (1) the percentage of people living in rural areas was greater than the percentage of people living in urban areas.

    (2) the percentage of people living in urban areas was greater than the percentage of people living in rural areas.

    (3) the percentage of people living in urban areas continued to decline.

8. In 1880 most people lived in

    (1) urban areas.

    (2) familiar environments.

    (3) rural areas.

Questions 9–11 are based on the following passage.

During World War I many women and minorities were enlisted into the United States military. Some women served as clerks in the navy and army. Some female nurses were taken into the army. About 400,000 black men were drafted or enlisted into the military. They were kept in segregated (or all-black) units. Some black units saw combat and a few black soldiers became officers of black units.

9. During World War I women served as

    (1) soldiers in the army.

    (2) nurses and clerks in the military.

    (3) clerks and soldiers.

10. What kind of units were the black soldiers a part of?

    (1) All-black units.

    (2) Desegregated units.

    (3) Units that included women.

11. A few black soldiers became

    (1) nurses.

    (2) tired of the military.

    (3) officers.

Questions 12–14 are based on the following passage.

Anarchism emerged in the early 1800s. Anarchism is the theory that argues for living without property or authority. One famous anarchist, Pierre Proudhon, said that anarchism could be achieved without violence. Another famous anarchist, Mikhail Bakunin, believed that anarchism could only be achieved with violence.

12. When did anarchism emerge?

    (1) In the 20th century.

    (2) In the medieval period.

    (3) In the early 1800s.

13. Which best describes the theory of anarchism?

    (1) Property and authority should be lived without.

    (2) People should increase property holdings.

    (3) People should love each other more.

14. Bakunin said that he believed that anarchism could only be achieved through violence. This is considered a(n)

    (1) fact.

    (2) opinion.

    (3) false statement.

Questions 15–17 are based on the following passage.

Louis XIV of France reigned from 1643 until 1715. He is one of the most famous kings in history. Louis believed in the absolute, unquestioned authority of the crown. He was also vain and arrogant. Louis moved his palace from Paris to Versailles, 12 miles outside of Paris. There he spent 60% of the royal tax revenue on the upkeep of the palace and on amusements such as dinners, operas, and parties for himself. In order to celebrate the birth of his son in 1662 he arranged a party that was attended by 15,000 people.

15. Louis XIV moved his palace

    (1) from Versailles to Paris.

    (2) out of France.

    (3) from Paris to Versailles.

16. The spending habits of the king could best be described as

    (1) careful.

    (2) extravagant.

    (3) controlled.

17. Louis believed in absolute, unquestioned authority of the crown. This means

    (1) he listened to the opinions of other Frenchmen.

    (2) many people told him how to rule France.

    (3) people could not question how he ruled the country.

Questions 18–20 are based on the following passage.

There were several factors that led to the Great Depression that began in the 1920s. First, wages did not increase enough to keep up with industrial output. As a result, people did not buy enough goods and the factories built up inventories. Second, layoffs and further decreases in spending occurred. Third, the stock market crashed in 1929.

18. Which event occurred second?

    (1) The Great Depression.

(2)   The stock market crashed.

(3)   Layoffs and further decreases in spending occurred.

19.   Which of the following is an example of cause and effect?

(1)   Layoffs and decreases in spending led to decreases in wages.

(2)   The factories built up their inventories once the Great Depression occurred.

(3)   The lack of an increase in real wages caused a decline in the amount of goods people bought.

20.   Which of the following was the effect of wages not keeping up with output, layoffs, factories building up inventories, and the stock market crash?

(1)   The Great Depression.

(2)   An increase in layoffs.

(3)   People were becoming rich.

Questions 21 and 22 are based on the following passage.

After the American Revolution women were asked to take on the responsibility of becoming "republican mothers." This meant that women were to teach their sons the virtues of truth, a sense of public service, honor, and wisdom. In this way women could enter public life through their sons instead of directly. Women were not granted the right to vote, hold public office, or teach in public schools.

21.   What were women asked to do after the American Revolution?

(1)   Have more children.

(2)   Teach their sons many virtues.

(3)   Teach in public schools.

22.   By inferring, or applying meanings, what other rights do you assume women were not granted?

(1)   The right to have more children.

(2)   The right to publish articles on politics.

(3)   The right to teach virtues to their children.

Questions 23 and 24 are based on the following cartoon.

HORRID MASSACRE IN VIRGINIA

23.   The title of the cartoon means

(1)   a war occurred in Virginia.

(2)   a massive fire occurred in Virginia.

(3)   many people were killed in Virginia.

24.   The artist of the cartoon thinks that

(1)   the people labeled "1" and "2" are the victims.

(2)   the people labeled "1" and "2" are the attackers.

(3)   the people labeled "1" and "2" deserved to be killed.

Questions 25–27 are based on the following passage.

American immigration from 1870 until 1914 grew at a fast rate. Most of the new immigrants came from Southern and Eastern Europe, as well as Russia. They came to America seeking religious and political freedom. After 1914 Congress drastically reduced the number of immigrants allowed into America.

25. During which years did American immigration grow quickly?

    (1) 1880 until 1914.

    (2) 1870 until 1914.

    (3) 1870 until 1916.

26. What caused people to immigrate to America?

    (1) They were looking for work.

    (2) They wanted to be free from politics.

    (3) They were looking for religious and political freedom.

27. What can you infer about the location of Russia?

    (1) It is not in Southern or Eastern Europe.

    (2) It is near New York.

    (3) It is in Southern Europe.

Questions 28 and 29 are based on the following passage.

In 1932 Franklin Roosevelt became President of the United States. Roosevelt was born in 1882, graduated from Harvard and Columbia Law School, married his distant cousin Anna Eleanor Roosevelt in 1905, and practiced law in New York City. In 1928 he was elected governor of New York and was reelected in 1930.

28. Franklin Roosevelt

    (1) graduated from law school and then went to Harvard.

    (2) served only one term as governor of New York.

    (3) married his distant cousin.

29. What should be inferred about Roosevelt's education?

    (1) He had little education.

    (2) He was self-educated.

    (3) He had an excellent education at top schools.

Questions 30 and 31 are based on the following passage.

The President of the United States is elected for a four-year term. Although originally electable without limit, the 22nd Amendment now limits the time served by one person as President to two terms. Responsibilites for the President as outlined in the Constitution include acting as Chief of State, the Chief Executive, Commander-in-Chief of the Armed Forces, the Chief Diplomat, and Chief Legislator.

30. For how long is one term of the Presidency of the United States?

    (1) Two years.

    (2) Four years.

    (3) Eight years.

31. Which of the following responsibilities gives the President the power to command the Army, Navy, Air Force, and Marines?

    (1) Chief of State.

    (2) Chief of Legislature.

    (3) Commander-in-Chief of the Armed Forces.

Question 32 refers to the following table.

State	Student Dropout Rate
Connecticut	17.8%
Iowa	13.1%
Massachusetts	30.1%
Michigan	27.1%
Missouri	24.5%
New York	33.7%
Tennessee	31.4%
Texas	35.1%
Wisconsin	16.7%

32. Which of the following statements do we know is true?

    (1) Texas has the highest dropout rate.

    (2) New York has the highest dropout rate.

    (3) Wisconsin has the lowest dropout rate.

SOCIAL STUDIES

ANSWER KEY

1. (2)	9. (2)	17. (3)	25. (2)
2. (3)	10. (1)	18. (3)	26. (3)
3. (1)	11. (3)	19. (3)	27. (1)
4. (3)	12. (3)	20. (1)	28. (3)
5. (1)	13. (1)	21. (2)	29. (3)
6. (2)	14. (2)	22. (2)	30. (2)
7. (2)	15. (3)	23. (3)	31. (3)
8. (3)	16. (2)	24. (1)	32. (1)

PRE-TEST SELF-EVALUATION

Question Number	Subject Matter Tested	Section to Study (section, heading)
1.	reading comprehension	II
2.	reading comprehension	II
3.	reading comprehension	II
4.	important details	II, Asking Who, What, Where, and When
5.	reading comprehension	II
6.	facts and opinions	IV, Distinguishing Fact from Opinion
7.	reading graphs	V, Applying Information from Graphs
8.	reading graphs	V, Applying Information from Graphs
9.	reading comprehension	II
10.	reading comprehension	II
11.	reading comprehension	II
12.	reading comprehension	II
13.	reading comprehension	II
14.	fact or opinion	IV, Distinguishing Fact from Opinion
15.	reading comprehension	II
16.	reading comprehension	II, Using Context to Figure Out Unfamiliar Words
17.	reading comprehension	II, Using Context to Figure Out Unfamiliar Words
18.	recognizing sequences	IV, Identifying Sequences
19.	cause and effect	IV, Cause and Effect Relationships
20.	cause and effect	IV, Cause and Effect Relationships
21.	reading comprehension	II
22.	inference	IV, Inferring Meanings
23.	political cartoons	II, Using Context Clues to Understand Unfamiliar Words V, Applying Information from Political Cartoons
24.	political cartoons	V, Applying Information from Political Cartoons
25.	reading comprehension	II
26.	reading comprehension	II
27.	inference	IV, Inferring Meanings

II = Comprehending What You Read   III = Graphs and Charts   IV = Reading Patterns   V = Applying Information

Question Number	Subject Matter Tested	Section to Study (section, heading)
28.	reading comprehension	II
29.	inference	IV, Inferring Meaning
30.	reading comprehension	II
31.	reading comprehension, inference	II, IV
32.	reading comprehension, reading graphs	II, III

PRE-TEST
ANSWERS AND EXPLANATIONS

1. **(2)** Read the first sentence to find the correct answer. Choices (1) and (3) are branches of the federal government but are not mentioned in this passage.

2. **(3)** Read the first sentence to find the correct answer. Choice (1) is an opinion, not a fact and Choice (2) is incorrect since the passage states that a person running for President has to be a natural born citizen of the United States.

3. **(1)** The correct answer can be found in the sentence that reads, *Any person running for President must be at least thirty-five years old and be a natural born citizen of the United States.* All of the other choices are untrue.

4. **(3)** The correct answer can be found in the first sentence of the passage. Neither of the other responses are mentioned in the passage.

5. **(1)** The correct answer can be found in the second sentence of the passage, which reads, *The next year gold-seekers from the eastern United States and many foreign countries went to California seeking gold.*

6. **(2)** The correct answer can be found in the first sentence of the passage. Choices (1) and (3) are opinions, not facts.

7. **(2)** The number of people living in urban areas was greater. The solid line represents people who live in urban areas. That line, when it corresponds with the year 1980, is at the 72% or 73% mark. The dotted line represents the number of people who live in rural areas. In 1980 that number was only about 25%. Choice (3) is incorrect since the percentage is actually on the rise.

8. **(3)** The correct answer can be found by looking at where the dotted line begins, which would be the year 1880. In this case, it begins at 70%. The only other possible correct choice would be urban areas. That is an incorrect choice because only about 30% of the population lived in urban areas in 1880.

9. **(2)** The correct answer can be found in two lines from the passage. These two lines read, *Some women served as clerks in the army and navy. Some female nurses were taken into the army.* None of the other choices are mentioned in the passage.

10. **(1)** The answer can be found in the sentence that reads, *They were kept in segregated, (or all-black) units.* None of the other choices are mentioned.

11. **(3)** The correct answer can be found in the last sentence, which reads, *Some black units saw combat and a few black soldiers became officers of black units.* None of the other choices are mentioned.

12. **(3)** The correct answer can be found in the first sentence, which reads, *Anarchism emerged in the early 1800s.* None of the other choices are mentioned.

13. **(1)** The correct answer can be found in the sentence that reads, *Anarchism is the theory that argues for living without property or authority.* None of the other choices are mentioned.

14. **(2)** Bakunin was giving his opinion. The word "believed" gives the clue that he was giving an opinion. Facts can be proved right or wrong, opinions cannot.

15. **(3)** The correct answer can be found in the sentence that reads, *Louis moved his palace from Paris to Versailles, 12 miles outside of Paris.* Choice (1) describes where he moved the palace from. Choice (2) is the country in which Louis lived.

16. **(2)** The correct answer can be found in the last two sentences of the passage where the king's habit of spending a lot of money is described. Choices (1) and (3) are untrue, and they both have similar meanings.

17. **(3)** "Absolute" means "total." "Unquestioned authority" means no one can question his power.

18. **(3)** The correct answer can be found in the sentence that reads, *Second, layoffs and further decreases in spending occurred.* Choice (2) happened third and choice (1) occurred last.

19. **(3)** Since wages did not go up people did not buy as much. Choice (1) is incorrect since layoffs and decreases in spending happened after the decrease in wages. Choice (2) is incorrect since factories building up inventories led to the Great Depression, so they could not have happened simultaneously.

20. **(1)** Wages not keeping up with output, layoffs, factories building up inventories, and the stock market crash were the causes of the Great Depression. Therefore, the effect of the above events was the Great Depression.

21. **(2)** The answer can be found in the sentences that read, *After the American Revolution women were asked to take on the responsibility of becoming "republican mothers." This meant that women were to teach their sons the virtues of truth, a sense of public service, honor, and wisdom.* Choices (1) and (3) are not mentioned.

22. **(2)** If women were not given the right to hold public office or vote, they were probably not given the right to publish articles about politics. Choice (1) is incorrect because the article infers the opposite, that having children is a proper duty. Choice (3) is incorrect, the passage directly refutes it.

23. **(3)** The title of the cartoon, *A Horrid Massacre in Virginia*, means a terrible series of killings in Virginia.

24. **(1)** Choice (1) is correct because the people labeled "1" and "2" are kneeling down on the ground with their hands up in protest or trying to protect themselves. The attackers are standing over people "1" and "2" with weapons in their hands. Choice (3) is a statement that cannot be inferred and is one that is very unlikely.

25. **(2)** The correct answer can be found in the first sentence, which reads, *American immigration from 1870 until 1914 grew at a fast rate.*

26. **(3)** The correct answer can be found in the sentence that reads, *They came to America seeking religious and political freedom.* Choice (1) could be true but it is not mentioned in the passage. Choice (2) is incorrect since the people wanted to have political freedom, not to live completely without politics.

27. **(1)** The correct answer can be found in the sentence that reads, *Most of the new immigrants came from Southern and Eastern Europe, as well as Russia.* The sentence is implying, or inferring, that Russia is not in either Southern or Eastern Europe.

28. **(3)** The correct answer can be found in the second sentence which, in listing the things that Roosevelt did, states that he married his distant cousin. Choice (1) is incorrect since

Roosevelt graduated college from Harvard and then went to Columbia Law School. Choice (2) is incorrect because we know that Roosevelt was elected to a second term as governor.

29. **(3)**   The passage says that Roosevelt attended Harvard and Columbia Law School. Even if you have not heard of the schools, you know that Roosevelt attended college and law school. The only choice that corresponds to his having attended college and law school is choice (3).

30. **(2)**   The correct answer can be found in the first part of the first sentence, which reads *is elected for a four-year term.*

31. **(3)**   The correct choice is Commander in Chief of the Armed Forces because it is the only answer choice that deals with the Army, Navy, Air Force, and Marines, which are collectively known as the Armed Forces.

32. **(1)**   Texas has the highest dropout rate of 35.1%.

Comprehending What You Read

SOCIAL STUDIES

COMPREHENDING WHAT YOU READ

In this chapter you will learn how to approach a new passage. The first step is to *preview the paragraph*. This important step lets your brain activate. The second step is to read the passage and find the *main idea* and *supporting ideas* of the passage. This tells you what the passage is about. The third step is to think about what you knew about the passage *before* you read it and what you learned *by* reading it. This makes your brain focus on the issues of the passage. The fourth step is to ask yourself *who, what, where,* and *when.* These are essential to understanding the details of the paragraph. The fifth and final step is to use *context clues* that help you to figure out the meaning of words that you did not know. Words that you do not understand may be essential to answering a question correctly.

PREVIEWING PARAGRAPHS

Before beginning to read, an essential and helpful point in understanding and absorbing is to preview the material. *Previewing* simply means looking over an article to see what it is about before you begin to read. There are three ways in which this is done. The first is to read the first sentence, the second is to recognize repeated words, and the third is to glance at the capitalized words.

Glance at the following passage and then answer the questions that follow.

The American Civil War was fought between the years 1861 and 1865. Many people refer to this war as the War Between the States. The war was fought between the Northern states, called the Union, and the Southern states, called the Confederacy. The most famous figures of the war were President Abraham Lincoln, Robert E. Lee, and Ulysses S. Grant. The war took more American lives than any other war in U.S. history. It also ended the institution of slavery in America.

Questions

1. Did you notice that a word seems to be repeated several times? What word is it?

_____

2. What words are capitalized?

_____

3. What is the first sentence of the passage?

_____

Answers

1. The word *war* is repeated several times. If you did not notice this, glance again at the passage. The word is used in every sentence.

2. Several words are capitalized, including *American, Civil, War, Union, Confederacy,* and *Lincoln.* It is important to notice capitalized words because they tell you a lot about the passage. For instance, in this case, the capitalized words tell you that the passage is about the American Civil War.

3. The first sentence is: *The American Civil War was fought between the years 1861 and 1865.* Glancing at the first sentence is helpful because it, too, tells you what the passage is about.

Here is another passage for your practice in previewing paragraphs. Only glance at the passage, do not read it. The object of this exercise is to save time by learning something about the paragraph before actually reading it.

> The American federal government is composed of three branches. The legislative branch has two separate bodies of elected officials, the Senate and the House of Representatives. Each state has two Senators and each state has Representatives based on their population. Another branch of the federal government is the judicial branch. This branch contains the Supreme Court only. Members of the court are nominated by the President and approved by the Senate. The final branch of the federal government is the executive branch, which refers to the President's office. The President is elected by the citizens of the United States.

Questions

1. What is the first sentence of the paragraph?

   _____

2. What words are capitalized?

   _____

3. What words are repeated?

   _____

Answers

1. The first sentence reads: *The American federal government is composed of three branches.*

2. The words *American, Senate, House of Representatives, Senators, Supreme Court, President,* and *United States* are some of the capitalized words.

3. The words *federal, branch,* and *government* are repeated several times.

Again, previewing a paragraph can be very helpful in learning quickly what a passage is about without reading it. It is a useful first step when confronted with a new passage.

Glance at the following paragraph and make some guesses as to what the passage is about. You can do this by reading the first sentence, recognizing repeated words, and recognizing the capitalized words. You should also look at any words in italics or bold print.

> The United States won its independence from Britain in what is known as the American Revolution. The revolution was fought between 1775 and 1783. The fighting first broke out at Lexington and Concord. George Washington was made Commander of the Continental Army by the

Continental Congress. On July 4, 1776, the Declaration of Independence was adopted as the statement of American independence from Britain. The fighting ended with the surrender of General Cornwallis in October of 1781, and the Treaty of Paris recognized the United States as a nation.

Questions

1. What is the first sentence of the passage?

    _____

2. What words are repeated?

    _____

3. What words are capitalized?

    _____

Answers

1. The first sentence is: *The United States won its independence from Britain in what is known as the American Revolution.*

2. The words *United States, revolution,* and *fighting* are repeated.

3. The words *United States, Britain, Washington,* and *Treaty* are some of the words that are capitalized.

What did the above questions tell you about the passage? They told you that it was about the American Revolution. The repeated words and the capitalized words mentioned the United States, Britain, and revolution. When these words are used together in a short paragraph it probably means that the paragraph is about the American Revolution. The first sentence clearly states that the passage is about the American Revolution.

Let's try one last example for previewing paragraphs. Again, glance at the passage, read the first sentence, and then answer the questions that follow.

There is currently a debate among parents and schools in America over corporal punishment. Corporal punishment, also known as spanking, has made a resurgence in some schools in the last five years. Some parents are supportive of the schools' decisions to punish children in this manner. The parents who support corporal punishment say that (when done correctly) it does not physically harm the child at all, but forces the child to stop his/her bad behavior. Other parents are appalled at the resurgence of this type of punishment and say that it only frightens children. Some opponents even call it child abuse. This debate will probably not end soon, but will instead grow more heated.

Questions

1. What is the first sentence of the paragraph?

    _____

2. What words are repeated?

    _____

3. What words are capitalized?

    _____

Answers

1. The first sentence is: *There is currently a debate among parents and schools in America over corporal punishment.*

2. The words *debate, parents, schools, corporal,* and *punishment* are repeated.

3.   The words *corporal, some,* and *other* are some of the capitalized words.

FINDING THE MAIN IDEA

Another key to understanding a passage is to recognize the *main idea* of that passage. This usually involves reading the passage and then re-reading the first sentence. In many cases the first sentence contains the main idea, but not always. When the main idea can be found in a single sentence it is called a *topic sentence.* Sentences that help you understand the topic sentence are called *supporting sentences.*

You will understand the process of finding

main ideas and supporting sentences better if you try it yourself. Read the following passage and then answer the questions that follow.

> Mary's favorite thing in the world is flowers. Because of her love for flowers she knows a lot about them. She not only knows the names of many flowers, but she also knows the names of the most famous flower growers.

Questions

1.   What is the main idea?

_____

_____

_____

2.   What are the supporting sentences?

_____

_____

_____

Answers

1.   The first sentence, which reads *Mary's favorite thing in the world is flowers,* is the main idea.

2.   The second and third sentences in the paragraph are the supporting sentences. They support the idea that Mary's favorite thing is flowers by explaining how much she loves them.

Here is a paragraph about world history. Find the main idea and the supporting sentences.

> The great empire of Rome was perhaps the greatest of all ancient cultures. The Romans had museums, libraries, and theatres. Great statesmen, businessmen, poets, artists, and even historians made up part of Roman society. Some women were able to be important Roman citizens and ran their own businesses. Ancient Rome even had modern infrastructure like sewage systems, roads, and fire departments.

Questions

1. What is the main idea? Is it contained in one topic sentence?

   _____

   _____

   _____

2. What do you think is/are the supporting sentence(s)?

   _____

   _____

   _____

Answers

1. The main idea is contained in the first sentence of the paragraph and is contained in one topic sentence. The main idea is: *The great empire of Rome was perhaps the greatest of all ancient cultures.*

   The first sentence of the above paragraph is the main idea because it is the big statement that all of the other sentences support. The other sentences give details about why Rome was a great empire, whereas the first sentence offers a general statement about Rome that sets up what the paragraph will be about.

2. The supporting sentences are the sentences following the first sentence. They are: *The Romans had museums, libraries, and theatres. Great statesmen, businessmen, poets, artists, and even historians made up part of Roman society. Some women were able to be important Roman citizens and ran their own businesses. Ancient Rome even had modern infrastructure like sewage systems, roads, and fire departments.*

The above answer is correct because the following sentences all explain more about the topic sentence. They give more information about why Rome was a great ancient culture. They do not discuss other topics.

Here is a different passage. Read it and then answer the questions that follow about main ideas and supporting sentences.

Whether or not President Truman was right to use the atomic bomb on Japan in 1945 has been a topic of debate for many years. Some people do not think that the action was justified. They believe that the use of the bomb was brutal and cruel. They believe that Japan would have surrendered soon anyway. Most people, however, seem to agree with Truman's decision. These people believe that many more American lives would have been lost if the U.S. had not dropped the bomb on Japan and ended World War II abruptly. Because of Truman's decision, it is now a part of history that the first atomic bomb was dropped on the city of Hiroshima on August 6, 1945, and the second atomic bomb was dropped on the city of Nagasaki on August 9, 1945. The Japanese formally surrendered on September, 2, 1945, on the deck of the battleship *Missouri*.

Questions

1. What is the main idea of the passage?

   _____

   _____

   _____

2. What is/are the supporting sentence(s)?

   _____

   _____

   _____

Answers

1. The main idea is, *Whether or not President Truman was right to use the atomic bomb on Japan in 1945 has been a topic of debate for many years.*

    The above sentence is the main idea and topic sentence because it contains the central point of the article.

2. There are several supporting sentences, starting at the second sentence and ending with the sixth sentence. They read, *Some people do not think that the action was justified. They believe that the use of the bomb was brutal and cruel. They believe that Japan would have surrendered soon anyway. Most people, however, seem to agree with Truman's decision. These people believe that many more American lives would have been lost if the U.S. had not dropped the bomb on Japan and ended World War II abruptly.* These sentences explain the debate over Truman's decision in greater detail.

    Let's try another example. Read the following passage and then look for the main idea, which might be in the form of a topic sentence, and look for the supporting sentences.

> Older children often ask their teachers what the bubonic plague was and how people got it. Teachers can now answer them with some confidence. Historians know quite a bit about the origin and nature of the plague. The bubonic plague, or Black Death, is a disease that affects the lymph glands. When a person is infected, he/she dies quickly. In 14th century Europe the plague was carried by fleas from black rats that had been brought from Asia by merchants. It spread very rapidly because living conditions allowed it to. There was no urban sanitation and the streets were filled with dead animals and excrement. Overcrowding and poor nutrition were also problems.

Questions

1. What is the main idea or topic sentence of the passage?

    _____

    _____

    _____

2. What are the supporting sentences?

    _____

    _____

    _____

Answers

1. The main idea is: *Historians know quite a bit about the origin and nature of the plague.* This is the main idea for the following reasons. The first two sentences talk about students and teachers and questions about the plague. If the rest of the paragraph were about how teachers address those concerns then the first or second sentence would be the main idea. Instead, the passage gives details about the bubonic plague. The third sentence sets up what the rest of the passage is about, that is why it is the topic sentence.

2. The sentences following the third sentence are the supporting sentences. Each one directly addresses what historians know about the origins and nature of the bubonic plague.

    Let's try one last example. Read the following article and then answer the questions that follow.

> The Republican party has been through many ups and downs in American history.

The Republican party was founded in 1854 by men who opposed slavery being extended into new American territory. A famous Republican who helped the party was President Lincoln. Republicans dominated the South until the election in 1876 of President Rutherford B. Hayes. During Republican Herbert Hoover's presidency, the party was blamed for the Great Depression. They then lost every election between 1932 and 1952. President Nixon hurt the party because of the Watergate scandal in 1972. Popular Republican presidents include Ronald Reagan, George H.W. Bush, and George W. Bush.

Questions

1. What is the main idea of the passage?

    _____

    _____

    _____

2. What are the supporting sentences?

    _____

    _____

    _____

Answers

1. The first sentence of the passage represents the main idea because it introduces it and covers the major points of the passage.

2. All of the sentences besides the first and second sentence support the main idea of the passage, that is, they discuss either a good period or a bad period of Republican history. The second sentence only states when the party was founded.

THINKING ABOUT THE TOPIC

Once you know what the main idea of a passage is, you can begin to think about what you *already know* about the topic before reading it. Draw on your wide variety of experiences to think about what you have heard or read about a subject. You might not know very much about the subject, but any knowledge can help you to answer questions correctly.

It is helpful to think about the topic *after* establishing what the main idea is. That enables you to think specifically about the topic. Think about what you already know about a passage, then think about what *you have learned* about the subject by reading the passage.

The objective in this section is to get you thinking about the subject.

Read the passage that follows, and decide what the main idea is. Then think about what you already know about the subject, and what you have learned from reading the passage.

The Constitution of the United States gives the President many powers. The President is the Commander-in-Chief of the Army, Navy, Air Force, and Marines, an extremely important duty. The President has the power to appoint Supreme Court justices, although his choices have to be approved by the Senate. He/she also has the power to veto bills that Congress sends to him/her. Also, the President has the power to sign treaties with foreign countries.

Questions

1. What is the main idea or topic sentence of the paragraph?

    _____

    _____

    _____

2. What did you already know about the powers of the President before reading the paragraph?

    _____

    _____

    _____

3. What did you learn about the President's powers because of reading the article?

    _____

    _____

    _____

Answers

1. The main idea is the first sentence of the passage, which reads, *The Constitution of the United States gives the President many powers.*

2. Perhaps you knew only that the President was Commander-in-Chief. Perhaps you knew about all of his Constitutional powers.

3. You probably learned about some of the President's powers that you did not know about previously.

Remember, it is important to take this step after finding the main idea because that way you focus your thoughts on the specific subject at hand. This also allows you to think about what you previously knew and what you have learned in one quick step. *Thinking about what you have learned from a passage is key to answering questions about it in a rapid manner.*

Let's start from the top. When confronted with a new passage, first preview it. This gets your brain "in gear." Second, find the main idea and the supporting sentences. This tells you what the passage is about. Third, think about what you knew before reading the passage and what you have learned from it.

Read the following paragraph and use the first three steps to approach a new passage.

Karl Marx developed a communist philosophical system in the mid 19th century. Marx was a German philosopher who was born in 1818 and died in 1883. His most famous book, *The Communist Manifesto*, was written in 1848. His system was founded on the idea of the inherent goodness of man. He argued that men were basically good but had been corrupted by institutions like states and churches. Marx believed that the proletariat, or the industrial working class, had to be educated and led towards a violent revolution that would destroy these institutions. He also believed that the history of humanity was the history of class struggle, which would only end when a classless society existed.

Questions

1. When you previewed the passage what words seemed to repeat? What words were capitalized? Did you note what the first sentence was?

   _____

   _____

   _____

2. What is the main idea of the paragraph?

   _____

   _____

   _____

3. What did you know about the subject before you read it? What did you learn by reading it?

   _____

   _____

   _____

Answers

1. The words *Marx, institutions,* and *class* are repeated. The words *Karl, Marx, German, Communist,* and *Manifesto* are capitalized. The first sentence is: *Karl Marx developed a communist philosophical system in the mid 19th century.*

2. The main idea is the first sentence of the paragraph. It reads: *Karl Marx developed a communist philosophical system in the mid 19th century.* This sentence covers everything that the paragraph talks about. In other words, the rest of the paragraph gives supporting details about Marx's system.

3. Perhaps you had only heard that Karl Marx was a communist. The rest of the information in the passage might be new to you. Think about what the passage told you about Marx's work and his life.

   Here is a passage that will probably be on a subject familiar to most people. Glance at the paragraph to preview it. Then read the paragraph, find the main idea, and recall what you knew about the subject before reading and what you learned by reading the passage.

   Taxation is a system that allows the government to take money from its citizens to fund the government. The money is then used for a wide variety of purposes. Some money is used for public services like highways and roads. Some is used for social services like welfare, Medicare, and Social Security. Some is also used for maintaining the armed services and paying the salaries of government officials. Taxes are classified as proportional, progressive, or regressive.

Questions

1. When you glanced at the paragraph what words were repeated?

   _____

   _____

   _____

2. What is the main idea of the paragraph?

   _____

   _____

   _____

3. What did you know about taxation before reading the article?

_____

_____

_____

4. What did you learn about taxation that you did not know before reading the article?

_____

_____

_____

Answers

1. The words *taxation, money,* and *government* are some of the repeated words.

2. The main idea is in the first sentence, which, in this case, can also be called the topic sentence. It reads: *Taxation is a system that allows the government to take money from its citizens to help fund the government.*

3. Perhaps you knew only that part of your paycheck is given to the government. Perhaps you did not know that your taxes pay for services like welfare, Medicare, and Social Security.

4. Perhaps you learned that there are three types of taxes.

Let's try one last example before concluding this section. Read the following passage and then answer the questions that follow.

Some people refer to the Korean War as the "forgotten war." The Korean War was fought between the years 1950 and 1953. The United States became involved in the war in order to stop the spread of communism. The communist North Koreans invaded South Korea in 1950 and the

United Nations authorized its members, including the United States, to aid South Korea. The communist Chinese came to the aid of the North Koreans in October of 1950. General Douglas MacArthur was the UN commander until he was replaced by General Matthew B. Ridgeway. At the end of the war the two countries kept the earlier status quo.

Questions

1. What is the main idea of the paragraph?

_____

_____

_____

2. What did you know about the history of the war before reading the passage?

_____

_____

_____

3. What did you learn about the history of the war from the passage?

_____

_____

_____

Answers

1. The second sentence of the paragraph contains the main idea: *The Korean War was fought between the years 1950 and 1953.*

The first sentence could only contain the main idea if the rest of the paragraph explained (something like) how other wars are remembered, but the Korean War is forgotten. Instead, the passage talks about the history of the war, which is covered in the second sentence.

2. You might have heard of it, read about it, or perhaps you know someone who fought in it.

3. You might have learned that MacArthur was the UN commander.

In the next section you will continue to learn how to comprehend what you read. You will learn how to ask important questions that will help you understand details in a passage.

ASKING *WHO, WHAT, WHERE,* AND *WHEN*

After you have glanced at the paragraph, recognized the main idea, and thought about the specific topic, it is time to look closely at the important details. By asking *who* the article is about, *what* happens in the article, *where* the action takes place, and *when* it happens, you learn the most important details of the article.

Who?

Read the following short passage, find the main idea, and then answer the questions that follow.

The American president during the First World War was Woodrow Wilson. Wilson was born in 1856, in Staunton, Virginia, and died in 1924. He was the 28th President of the United States.

Questions

1. What is the main idea of the paragraph?

_____

_____

_____

2. Who is the paragraph about?

_____

_____

_____

3. What details does the paragraph tell about Woodrow Wilson?

_____

_____

_____

Answers

1. The main idea is *The American President during the First World War was Woodrow Wilson.*

2. The paragraph is about Woodrow Wilson.

3. The paragraph tells us when Wilson was born and where, when he died, and that he was the 28th president of the U.S.

By answering the question *who*, you discovered who the paragraph was about. The next step was to ask what details you learned about the subject of the paragraph.

What?

Read the short paragraph that follows, find the main idea, and then answer the questions that follow.

Franklin D. Roosevelt was an American President. He was President during the height of the "Great Depression" and during most of World War II. Roosevelt was a Democrat. Few people knew that Roosevelt was paralyzed as a result of polio. He is still a controversial figure since some think of him as a great President and others blame him for government interference.

Questions

1. What is the main idea of the paragraph?

   _____

   _____

   _____

2. What happened to Roosevelt himself?

   _____

   _____

   _____

3. What happened during Roosevelt's presidency?

   _____

   _____

   _____

Answers

1. The main idea of the paragraph is encompassed in the first sentence.

2. Roosevelt was paralyzed and he became a controversial figure.

3. The "Great Depression" and World War II.

   By asking *what*, you discovered "what" happened to Roosevelt personally and "what" happened during his presidency.

Where?

Read the short paragraph that follows, and then answer the subsequent questions.

During World War II a famous battle occurred on the island of Okinawa. The island of Okinawa is the largest of the Ryukyu Islands, a part of Japan located southwest of Kyushu. United States forces seized the island from the Japanese in June of 1945 after months of fighting. The Japanese lost 100,000 men in the battle and the Americans lost 48,000.

Questions

1. What is the main idea of the passage?

   _____

   _____

   _____

2. Where is the island of Okinawa?

   _____

   _____

   _____

3. Where was one place that the Americans fought during World War II?

   _____

   _____

   _____

Answers

1. The main idea is in the first sentence.

2. The island is located in the Ryukyu Islands, near Kyushu, Japan.

3. One place where the Americans fought was on the island of Okinawa, which is part of Japan.

   By asking the question *where*, you discovered one place where Americans fought during the Second World War and where the island of Okinawa is located.

When?

The last question to ask yourself when confronted with a new passage is the question "when." Read the following short passage, find the main idea, and answer the accompanying questions.

The Americans entered the Second World War after being attacked at Pearl Harbor. On December 7, 1941, the Japanese surprised the American ships, planes, and servicemen at Pearl Harbor with an early morning attack. Pearl Harbor is located on Oahu Island, Hawaii.

Questions

1. What is the main idea of the passage?

    _____

    _____

    _____

2. When was Pearl Harbor attacked?

    _____

    _____

    _____

3. Approximately when was World War II?

    _____

    _____

    _____

Answers

1. The main idea is in the first sentence of the paragraph.

2. December 7, 1941.

3. You know from the passage that the attack on Pearl Harbor brought the United States into the Second World War, also known as World War II. You also know that Pearl Harbor was attacked in 1941. You can then figure out that the Second World War took place in 1941, and possibly before and after that date. In fact, the dates of the war are 1939–1945.

By asking the question *when*, you discovered when Pearl Harbor was attacked, which tells you when America entered World War II. You also discovered at least one year in which the war took place.

Below is a passage from the *Federalist Papers* written by Alexander Hamilton in 1787. The *Federalist Papers* were a series of written arguments that helped to create the Constitution of the United States. Don't worry if you do not understand every word in the paragraph. This exercise is designed to teach you how to find the meaning of a difficult passage; you can find these answers even if you don't understand every word in the passage.

The wealth of nations depends upon an infinite variety of causes. Situation, soil, climate, the nature of the productions, the nature of the government, the genius of the citizens, the degree of information they possess, the state of commerce, of arts, of industry, these circumstances and many more, too complex, minute, or adventitious to admit of a particular specification, occasion differences hardly conceivable in the relative opulence and riches of different countries. The consequence clearly is that there can be no common measure of national wealth, and, of course, no general or stationary rule by which the ability of a state to pay taxes can be determined. The attempt, therefore, to regulate the contributions of the members of a confederacy by any such rule, cannot fail to be productive of glaring inequality and extreme oppression.

Questions

1. What is the main idea of the paragraph?

   _____

   _____

   _____

2. On what does the wealth of the nations depend?

   _____

   _____

   _____

3. Why can't there be a stationary rule as to how much the states will have to pay in taxes to the federal government?

   _____

   _____

   _____

4. When will there be a "glaring inequality"?

   _____

   _____

   _____

Answers

1. The main idea is the first sentence of the paragraph, which says that there are many causes that make a nation wealthy.

2. The wealth of nations depends on an "infinite" or unending variety of causes. This answer can be found in the first sentence.

3. There cannot be a stationary rule, because the consequence of variations in natural resources (e.g., soil differences) and variations

in things such as the "genius of its citizens" create different amounts of wealth for nations or states. Therefore, the states will be able to pay taxes according to how their economy is doing, and not according to a pre-set amount. The answer can be found in the combination of the second and third sentences. The phrase "stationary rule" can be found in the third sentence. Stationary means fixed or unchanging. Sometimes it is also used in reference to a "stationary bike" in a health club: a bicycle that does not move but stays in one place.

4. There will be a "glaring inequality," as the last sentence says, when the federal government tries to force states to pay a pre-set amount of taxes, no matter how the economy of each state is doing. The key idea is contained in the phrase "regulate the contributions of the members."

By answering the above questions you now know all of the important details about the paragraph.

Here is another example for you to try.

The Supreme Court decided an important case in 1954, called *Brown vs. Board of Education of Topeka*. This decision overturned an 1896 case called *Plessy vs. Ferguson*. The 19th century decision ruled that the state of Louisiana had the right to segregate blacks and whites in railway carriages if the carriages were "separate but equal." The court said that the 14th amendment mandated political but not social equality. The 20th century case disallowed segregation. The court said that the school board in Topeka, Kansas could not segregate children based on the equal protection clause in the 14th amendment to the U.S. Constitution. This case helped give strength to the civil rights movement of the 1950s.

Questions

1. Who decided an important case?

    _____

    _____

    _____

2. Who were the two court cases about?

    _____

    _____

    _____

3. What were the cases about?

    _____

    _____

    _____

4. Where were the cases tried?

    _____

    _____

    _____

5. Where did the events take place that created the later case?

    _____

    _____

    _____

6. When were the cases tried in the Supreme Court?

    _____

    _____

    _____

Answers

1. The Supreme Court Justices.

2. The two court cases were about blacks and whites, and if they should be segregated. The earlier case was about people who sit in railway carriages and the second case was about children who go to school.

3. The cases were about racial segregation and whether or not it was legal.

4. The cases were tried at the Supreme Court in Washington, D.C.

5. The events took place in Topeka, Kansas.

6. The earlier case was tried in 1896 and the later was tried in 1954.

By asking the questions *who, what, where,* and *when*, you discovered all of the important details about the Supreme Court cases discussed in the paragraph.

Let's try one last example. Read the paragraph and then answer the questions that follow.

One group of American Indians is the Plains Indians. During the 18th century the American Plains Indians lived between the Mississippi River and the Rocky Mountains and from Southern Canada to Texas. There were Plains tribes that constantly moved from place to place, called nomadic tribes, and there were Plains tribes that stayed in one location, called sedentary tribes. The nomadic ones, like the Cheyenne, hunted buffalo and had many warrior clans. The sedentary ones, like the Pawnee, farmed the river valleys.

Questions

1. What is the main idea of the article?

   _____

   _____

   _____

2. Who is the article about?

   _____

   _____

   _____

3. What did the Plains Indians do to survive?

   _____

   _____

   _____

4. Where did the Indians live?

   _____

   _____

   _____

5. When did these tribes live in these areas and live like this?

   _____

   _____

   _____

Answers

1. The main idea is the first sentence of the paragraph, it covers what the rest of the paragraph will talk about.

2. The article is about the American Plains Indians.

3. The nomadic tribes hunted buffalo and the sedentary tribes farmed the river valleys.

4. The Indians lived between the Mississippi River and the Rocky Mountains and between Southern Canada and Texas.

5. The tribes lived in this area in the 18th century.

By asking four essential questions of the above paragraph you learned all of the important details that the author mentions. This will help you to understand the article better and to answer questions correctly on the GED test.

USING CONTEXT CLUES TO UNDERSTAND UNFAMILIAR WORDS

There may be instances during the GED test when you are confronted with words that you do not understand. Because dictionaries cannot be used, you need to find other ways to figure out the meanings of unfamiliar words. You might have observed how children learn words. They seem to learn by osmosis, or by getting the meaning of the word by how it fits with other words. Adults can learn new words in the same way. Let's start by using examples from passages already presented in this chapter.

The following sentence is from a passage about the three branches of the U.S. federal government.

> Another branch of the federal government is the judicial branch. This branch contains the Supreme Court only. Members of the court become Supreme Court justices because they are nominated by the President and approved by the Senate.

U.S. Supreme Court

Questions

1. What does the word "judicial" mean?

_____

_____

_____

2. What does the word "nominated" mean?

_____

_____

_____

Answers

1. "Judicial" means of, or about, judges. Notice that both words contain the root "jud." If you did not know the word already you probably could have figured out its meaning by looking at the context in which it was written. For example, you know that the judicial branch contains the Supreme Court only. This means that the word must have something to do with courts and justices. You also probably know the word "justice." The word "justice" and the word "judicial" sound alike because they are related.

2. The word "nominated" or "to nominate" means to name someone to a position. In this case, it means that the president names someone that he would like to be on the court, and the Senate has to approve that person. If you

did not know what the word meant you could have figured it out by looking at its context. The sentence says that members of the court are _____ by the President and approved by the Senate. The blank could not be filled in with the word "elected" because it takes more than one person to elect someone. The blank could not be filled in with the word "fired" because firing someone does not have to be approved, it is just done. The correct definition seems to present itself if you look at the other choices. Also, the word "nominate" sounds a bit like the word "name," and is, in fact, from the same root. You might have guessed its meaning that way.

Try another example. This sentence is from a passage that you have seen already about the Korean War. Read it and then answer the question that follows.

> The communist North Koreans invaded South Korea in 1950 and the United Nations authorized members, including the United States, to aid South Korea.

Question

1. What does the word "authorized" mean?

_____

_____

_____

Answer

1. The word "authorized" means "to give official approval or power." In this case, the United Nations gave UN members official approval or power to fight in a war on the side of South Korea.

If you did not know the word you could have figured it out. You know that a war is taking place and you know that the United Nations is some type of body made up of a lot of nations. Countries like the United States wanted to aid non-communist countries like South Korea and you could have figured out that the UN was letting them or giving them the power to do so.

Here is an example from a passage about Franklin D. Roosevelt. Read it and then answer the questions that follow.

He is still a controversial figure since some think of him as a great president and others blame him for government interference.

Questions

1. What does the word "controversial" mean?

    _____

    _____

    _____

2. What does the word "interference" mean?

    _____

    _____

    _____

Answers

1. The word "controversial" means "something that is subject to a conflict or dispute." In this example, it means that people debate about Roosevelt and his policies. You could have gotten the meaning of the word by looking at the words that follow it. The sentence says that some people feel good about him and others feel bad about him. This suggests a conflict or debate about him.

2. The word "interference" means "to come between or to meddle." In this case, it means that Roosevelt has been blamed for causing too

much government influence in people's lives. This is a difficult example because the context leaves little help in figuring it out. One way to figure it out would be to think of football and the use of the word there. In football it is used to mean that the other team came between the receiver and the ball. This would be helpful knowledge in finding the meaning for the word in the sentence about Roosevelt.

Here is an example from a passage about the American Revolution that you saw earlier in this chapter. Read it and then answer the questions that follow.

The United States won its independence from Britain in what is known as the American Revolution. The revolution was fought between 1775 and 1783. The fighting first broke out at Lexington and Concord. George Washington was made commander of the Continental Army by the Continental Congress. On July 4, 1776, the Declaration of Independence was adopted as the statement of American independence from Britain. The fighting ended with the surrender of General Cornwallis in October of 1781, and the Treaty of Paris recognized the United States as a nation.

Questions

1. What does the word "adopted" mean?

    _____

    _____

    _____

2. What does the word "surrender" mean?

    _____

    _____

    _____

Answers

1. It means to "take as one's own." In this case, it means that the ideas in the Declaration of Independence were taken as the ideas that the United States would exist by. You could have guessed the meaning of the word by realizing that the Declaration of Independence is part of what we celebrate on the July 4th holiday and that we still regard its ideas highly. This means that we have taken on or accepted its ideas. You also might have guessed the word by thinking about "adopting" children, which means to take them into your family and treat as your own.

2. It means to "give up or abandon." In this case it means that General Cornwallis gave up in October of 1781 and let the other side win. It was possible to guess this because the passage makes it clear that the United States won the war because they succeeded in winning independence from Britain and became a country. If you guessed that Cornwallis fought for the British then you guessed that he either gave up or was defeated. If you guessed that Cornwallis fought for the Americans then you might not have guessed the meaning of the word. Guessing the meaning of the word from its context is not an exact science, but a tool. Oftentimes that tool is sufficient enough to figure out the meaning of the word, but not always.

Here is an example about the Supreme Court that you have already seen. You will be asked to find the meaning of the words "overturn" and "disallowed."

The Supreme Court decided an important case in 1954, called *Brown vs. Board of Education of Topeka.* This decision would overturn an 1896 case called *Plessy vs. Ferguson.* The 19th century decision ruled that the state of Louisiana had the right to segregate blacks and whites in railway carriages if they were "separate but equal." The court said that the 14th amendment mandated political but not social equality. The 20th century case disallowed segregation. The court said that the school board in Topeka, Kansas could not segregate based on the equal protection clause in the 14th amendment to the U.S. Constitution.

Questions

1. What does the word "overturn" mean?

_____

_____

_____

2. What does the word "disallowed" mean?

_____

_____

_____

Answers

1. The word "overturn" means "to turn over or to conquer." In this case, it means that the court made a new decision that made the earlier one no longer legal. This word could be figured out by looking at the words that surround it. Follow this line of thinking. You know that there are two cases: an old one and a new one. You also know that the old case said the segregation was legal and the new one said it was illegal. The meaning of the unknown word would then be something like "turn over."

2. The word "disallowed" or "disallow" means to "not allow or to refuse to allow." In this example, it means that the 20th century case said that segregation based on race would not be allowed or would not be OK. This could be figured out by looking at its context. You

know that the school board, after the case was decided, could not segregate. This tells you that the word "disallow" means something like "would not be legal." You can also guess the word's meaning by realizing how much it sounds like the word "allow," which is its opposite. The prefix "dis-" usually means "does not."

Now we will start using examples that you have not already seen. Read the following passage and answer the questions that accompany it.

The Vietnam War was fought in the 1960s and 1970s. In 1954 the country was divided along the 17th parallel. The communists were in the Northern part, and the non-communist Republic of Vietnam was in the Southern part. In 1964 the United States became engaged in a full-scale war to prevent the Republic of Vietnam from becoming communist. The Chinese and the Soviet Union aided the communists. The war ended in 1973 with a ceasefire and by 1975 the communists had united the entire country.

Question

1.   In the passage about the Vietnam War above, what does the word "engaged" mean?

_____

_____

_____

Answer

1.   It means "became involved" in. You have probably heard of people who become engaged to be married. This use of the word is similar. You could also figure out the meaning of the word by looking at its context. You know that the U.S. fought in the war, so it seems that you

would see that the meaning of the word would be something like "got into" or "became involved with."

Try the following example. Read the paragraph and then answer the questions that go along with it.

Harriet Beecher Stowe's novel, *Uncle Tom's Cabin*, is an anti-slavery novel. Stowe, a religious Christian, was offended by the institution of slavery and believed that it was immoral. Written in 1852, just nine years before the inception of the Civil War, the book greatly raised anti-slavery sentiment. It is rumored that when President Lincoln met her in the mid 1860s he said, "So this is the little lady that caused this big war."

Questions

1.   What does the word "offended" mean?

_____

_____

_____

2.   What does the word "inception" mean?

_____

_____

_____

3.   What does the word "sentiment" mean?

_____

_____

_____

Answers

1.   It means to "create anger" or "cause offense." In this case, it means that the idea of slavery angered Stowe. You could figure this

out by realizing that she was an anti-slavery person, so slavery made her unhappy or angry.

2.   It means the "start" or "beginning" of something. Here it means that the book was written nine years before the Civil War started. This could be figured out by looking carefully at the sentence it is in. You know that the book was written nine years before the _____ of the Civil War. That blank would probably either include the word "start" or "end." It seems unlikely that someone would write a sentence that read, "the book was written nine years before the end of the Civil War."

3.   It means "feeling." In this example it means that the book caused anti-slavery feeling among people who read it. It seems that the phrase "raised anti-slavery _____" would mean either "anti-slavery feeling" or "anti-slavery awareness" or something along those lines. Another way to figure out the meaning of the word would be to think about what words sound like it. The word "sentimental" sounds like it and is close in meaning.

REVIEW

Many times reading passages on topics in social studies can seem very intimidating, and if we do not have a strategy for reading them, they can become very frustrating and confusing. In this chapter we covered four ways of approaching passages. They are:

- Previewing paragraphs

- Finding the main idea

- Asking *who*, *what*, *where*, and *when*

- Using context clues to understand details

Previewing paragraphs involves recognizing repeated words and capitalized words, and reading the first sentence. By doing this we are able to get a good idea of what the passage is concerned with before we begin reading. Previewing helps us comprehend passages because it has prepared our mind for what it is about to read, making it more receptive to the material.

Finding the main idea is a critical step in understanding social studies passages and will be a useful skill on the GED test. Many times the first sentence contains the main idea. Finding the main idea, or the topic sentence, involves putting all the details together and seeing which sentence best represents these ideas. Recognizing supporting sentences can also point you in the direction of the main idea.

Asking *who*, *what*, *where*, and *when* are skills critical in obtaining all the pertinent information in a passage. These are questions that are good to ask when seeking the complete answer to any passage.

Many times there are complex words that we do not understand in a passage. It is important to develop the skill of using context clues to understand details. This is a skill that will always be useful to you because there will always be words that you find difficult to understand and you will have to figure out what they mean by reading the words in the context they appear. Although you should look up words that you are not familiar with in a dictionary, you will not have a dictionary available when you are taking the GED.

Now answer the following questions based on the skills you have learned in this chapter.

☞ Practice: Comprehending What You Read

DIRECTIONS: Read the following passages. Apply the strategies you've learned. Write in the margins and mark up the text as you go. Then answer the questions following each passage.

One of the most famous days of the Second World War was D-Day, June 6, 1944. This day was the beginning of the final Allied campaign in Europe. Allied troops, led by the Americans, landed on the beaches in Normandy, which is in northwest France and borders the English Channel. The troops were led by American General Dwight D. Eisenhower. Other countries that participated in the Normandy invasion were Britain, Canada, Poland, and France. The now famous code name of the invasion was "Operation Overlord." The Allies attempted to liberate France from the Germans with the Normandy invasion and eventually succeeded in doing so.

1. When you previewed the passage what words seemed to repeat?

   _____

2. What words are capitalized?

   _____

3. What is the first sentence of the passage?

   _____

4. What is the main idea of the passage? Is it contained in one topic sentence?

   _____

5. What are the supporting sentences?

   _____

6. What did you know about D-Day or the Normandy invasion before you read the passage?

   _____

7. What have you learned about the subject by reading the passage?

   _____

8. Who participated in the invasion?

   _____

9. Who led the assault?

   _____

10. What happened on D-Day?

   _____

11. What was the result of the campaign?

   _____

12. Where did the Allies invade?

   _____

13. Where is Normandy, France?

   _____

14. When did D-Day occur?

   _____

15. What does the word "campaign" mean?

   _____

16. What does the word "liberate" mean?

   _____

Answers

1. The words *day, France, Normandy, Allies,* and *invasion* repeat.

2. The words *France, Normandy, Americans,* and *Allies* are some of the words that are capitalized.

3. The first sentence is: *One of the most famous days of the Second World War was D-Day, June 6, 1944.*

4. The main idea of the passage is the first sentence of the paragraph and is contained in that one sentence.

5. All of the sentences besides the first sentence are supporting sentences because they all describe D-Day, which is the topic of the paragraph.

6. Perhaps you knew only the name of the day and the name of the invasion, but not what their significance was. Perhaps you remember hearing about the 50th anniversary of D-Day. Perhaps a family member has told of being there or having a friend that was there.

7. You might have learned about the other countries that participated in the assault. You might have learned that Eisenhower was put in charge of the invasion. Perhaps you learned that Normandy is in northwest France.

8. The Allies participated in the invasion, including Americans, British, Canadians, Polish, and French.

9. The Americans led the assault under the guidance of General Eisenhower.

10. On D-Day, the Allies invaded France in order to liberate it from the Germans.

11. The invasion was eventually successful, and the Allies beat the Germans.

12. The Allies invaded on the beaches at Normandy, France.

13. Normandy, France is in northwest France, bordering the English Channel.

14. D-Day occurred on June 6, 1944.

15. It means "a series of military operations." In this example, it means that the Allied troops started one last group of military operations against the Germans. One hint that could help you figure out the meaning of the word would be to think about where you have seen "campaign" before. When someone wants to be elected, they "campaign" for office. There they have a series of appearances and planned actions in order to be elected. The two definitions are related and one could help you to find the other. In addition, you know that a military operation took place, so you are close to guessing the definition just by knowing that.

16. It means to "set free." In this case, it means that France was freed from the rule of the Nazis. You know that the aim was to free France from the Germans because the paragraph tells you so. That already helps you guess the word. You also might know that "liberals" usually want a freer society, another hint into the meaning of the word "liberate."

Graphs and Charts

SOCIAL STUDIES

GRAPHS AND CHARTS

In this chapter you will learn how to *preview* graphs and charts. Previewing graphs and charts is beneficial in the same way previewing was beneficial to comprehending what you read. Previewing begins the thinking process about a certain topic. You will then learn how to *get the main idea* from a graph or chart, an obviously important step. In the third and last section of this chapter you will learn how to *interpret the data* that you read from a graph or chart. This step enables you to put into words what you read from the graph or chart.

PREVIEWING GRAPHS

Glance at the following chart. Answer the questions that follow.

Questions

1. What words are repeated?

_____

2. What numbers are on the graph?

_____

3. What is the title of the graph?

_____

Answers

1. The words *household*, *discretionary income*, *college*, and *graduate* are repeated.

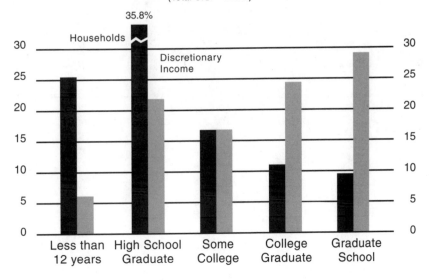

Education of Household Head

Percent Distribution of Households and Discretionary Income
(Total U.S. = 100%)

Educational Attainment

2. The numbers 0–30 are on the graph, in increments of five.

3. The title of the graph is: *Education of Household Head.*

We will return to the graph on the previous page later. First let's try more examples of previewing graphs and charts.

Glance at the following graph. Then answer the questions that accompany the graph.

Age of Household Head

Percent Distribution of Households and Discretionary Income
(Total U.S. = 100%)

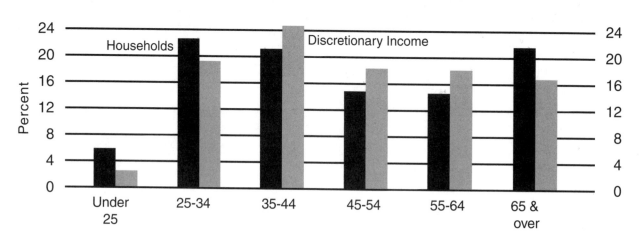

Questions

1. When you glanced at the graph what words are repeated?

_____

2. What numbers are repeated?

_____

3. What is the title of the graph?

_____

Answers

1. The words *household, discretionary income,* and *percent* are repeated.

2. The numbers: 0, 4, 8, 12, 16, 20, and 24 repeat.

3. The title of the graph is: *Age of Household Head.*

Here is another example. Glance at the chart below and then answer the questions that follow.

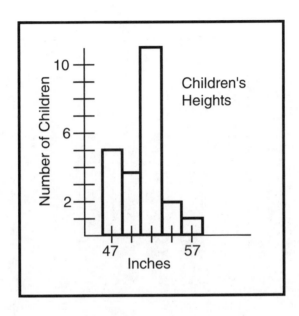

Questions

1. When you glanced at the graph what words did you see?

_____

2. What numbers are present?

_____

Answers

1. You see the words *number of children, inches,* and *children's heights*. In cases like this one, where no words are repeated, simply look at whatever words are present.

2. The numbers one through ten are on the left side and the numbers 47 through 57 are written on the bottom.

Here is one last example of previewing. Glance at the chart below and then answer the questions that go with it.

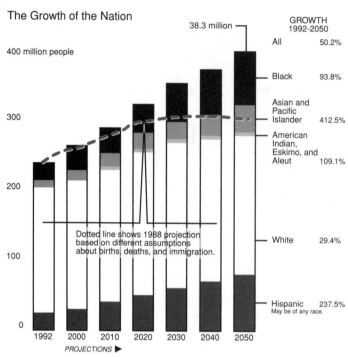

The Growth of the Nation

Questions

1. What words did you notice on or near the graph?

_____

2. What kinds of numbers did you notice?

_____

3. What is the title of the graph?

_____

Answers

1. You will see the words *growth*, *nation*, and *million*.

2. The numbers 0, 100, 200, 300, and 400 are on the left side. The dates 1992 and then 2000 through 2050 are on the bottom in 10 year increments.

3. The title is *The Growth of the Nation*.

Remember that previewing a graph or chart is very helpful because graphs and charts can be confusing. Previewing helps to get rid of the confusion. Always preview before trying to get the main idea of the graph or chart, which we will discuss in the next chapter.

Look closely at the following graph. Answer the question that follows.

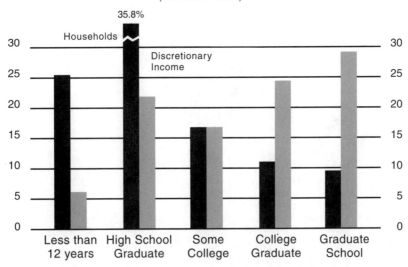

Education of Household Head

Percent Distribution of Households and Discretionary Income
(Total U.S. = 100%)

Question

1. What is the main idea of the graph?

_____

_____

_____

_____

_____

_____

_____

_____

Answer

1. The main idea of the graph is to show the relationship between how much education the head of a household has and how much discretionary income they have. You know this by first looking at the bottom of the graph where it says "educational attainment." Above that line are several educational levels, starting with "less than 12 years" and ending with "graduate school." That information tells you that the graph deals with groups of people who have different levels of education. Next, you look at the bars that are colored in black. You can see by the second one, where the word "households" is printed, that the black bars represent the number of households in percents. Lastly, look at the bars that are not colored in. You can see by looking at the second one where the words "discretionary income" are printed that the bars tell you how much discretionary income in percents that those households have. It is all right if you do not know what the word "discretionary" means for two reasons. The first reason is that you do not need to know it in order to discover the main idea. The second reason is that later on in this book we will practice again how to find the meaning of words that you do not know, but this time in graphs and charts.

Here is another graph that you saw in the previous section. Look at it closely in order to find the main idea.

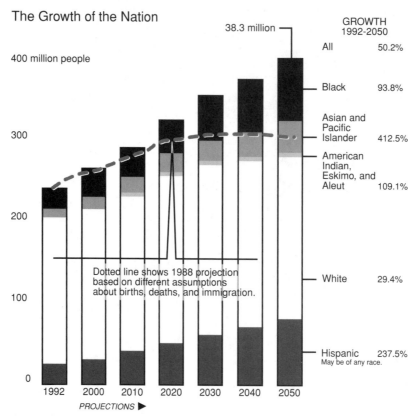

The Growth of the Nation

	GROWTH 1992-2050	
All	50.2%
Black	93.8%
Asian and Pacific Islander	412.5%
American Indian, Eskimo, and Aleut	109.1%
White	29.4%
Hispanic	237.5%
	May be of any race.

400 million people

300

200

100

0

1992 2000 2010 2020 2030 2040 2050

PROJECTIONS ▶

38.3 million —

Dotted line shows 1988 projection based on different assumptions about births, deaths, and immigration.

Question

1. What is the main idea of the graph?

_____

_____

_____

_____

_____

_____

_____

_____

Answer

1. The main idea is to show the possible population growth of different races of Americans in percents. You can see this by first looking at the bottom of the graph where the word "projections" is printed. Even if you do not know what the word "projection" means you can look at the years that are written above it and see what part of the main idea is about. There are dates written that start with a year in the past and go until a date that is years away in the future. This tells you that the graph has something to do with what could happen in the future. Next, look at the left side of the graph. Here it says 0–400 million people. This tells you that the graph has something to do with numbers of people. Next, look at the right side of the graph. Here it says "growth" and lists many races and percents. All of this information together tells you that the main idea is about growth, races, and what could happen in the future.

Try the following example. Look at the chart closely to find the main idea.

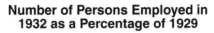

**Number of Persons Employed in
1932 as a Percentage of 1929**

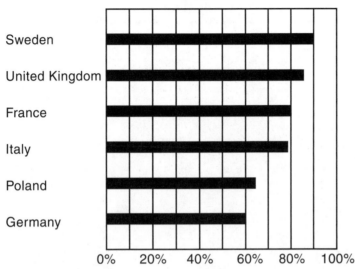

Question

1. What is the main idea of the chart?

_____

_____

_____

_____

_____

_____

_____

_____

Answer

1. This is a confusing and sophisticated chart, but you can still ascertain the main idea. The main idea is to show the number of people in certain European countries that were employed in 1929 and compare that number with the people employed in 1932. If you did not know the answer, you can follow this line of thinking. First, you can read the numbers on the bottom of the chart. They are percents, ranging from 0% to 100%. Next, read the left side of the chart. It lists six countries. Then read the top of the chart. It says, "Number of persons employed in 1932 as a percentage of 1929." Put those three facts together and you can see what the main idea is.

Try another chart example. Read the following closely in order to find the main idea.

Unemployment (Numbers in Thousands and Percentage of Appropriate Work Force)				
	Germany		Great Britain	
1930	3,076	15.3%	1,917	14.6%
1932	5,575	30.1%	2,745	22.5%
1934	2,718	14.9%	2,159	17.7%
1936	2,151	11.6%	1,755	14.3%
1938	429	2.1%	1,191	13.3%

Question

1. What is the main idea of the chart?

_____

_____

_____

_____

_____

_____

_____

_____

_____

_____

_____

_____

Answer

1. The main idea is to compare the unemployment rates in Germany and Great Britain in 1930 through 1938. The top of the chart, or its title, reads: *Unemployment (Numbers in Thousands and Percentage of Appropriate Work Force)*. This automatically tells you that the chart will deal with unemployment. Next, read the left hand column. There it gives several dates ranging from 1930 to 1938 in two-year increments. Next, read the names of the two countries on the chart. You will see that they are Germany and Great Britain. Finally, notice that there are both numbers and percentages, just like the title said there would be. Put all these facts together and you can see that the chart is about two countries and their unemployment rates from 1930 until 1938. When two countries are put together in one chart it is usually in order to compare them, like in this case.

Here is another example based on European history. "Urbanization" means the change from rural life to city life. The letters "ca." mean "circa" or "about." Read the graph closely and find the main idea.

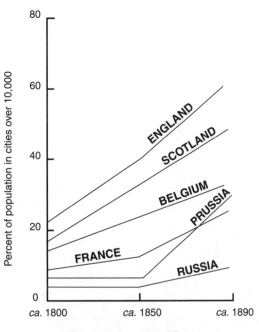

The Urbanization of Europe

Question

1. What is the main idea of the graph?

_____

_____

_____

_____

_____

_____

_____

_____

_____

Answer

1. The main idea is to show the change in the urbanization of six countries in the years 1800, 1850, and 1890. The title of the graph is at the bottom and says: *The Urbanization of Europe*. This automatically tells you that the graph is about urbanization. Next, look at the left side of the graph. It says: "percent of population in cities over 10,000." That means that the numbers up and down the left side of the graph refer to percent of people that live in cities of 10,000 people or more. Along the bottom there are three dates that tell you which years the graph pictures. Finally, look at the names of the six countries on the lines of the graph. Put all of this information together and you know that the graph deals with the growth of urban populations in six European countries from 1800 to 1890.

INTERPRETING DATA

In this section you will learn how to change the information on a chart or graph into words. A helpful aid in doing this is to ask *who, what, where,* and *when* in order to interpret the data.

Let's try each of these questions one at a time before mixing them all together. Look at the following and think about whom the chart describes.

STATE	Student Dropout Rate
Connecticut	17.8%
Iowa	13.1%
Massachusetts	30.1%
Michigan	27.1%
Missouri	24.5%
New York	33.7%
Tennessee	31.4%
Texas	35.1%
Wisconsin	16.7%

Question

1. Who is the chart talking about?

    _____

    _____

    _____

Answer

1. The chart is talking about people who drop out of school. You can discover this by looking at the right hand side of the chart. The top of that column says "Student Dropout Rate."

    The numbers on the right hand side tell you how many students, in percents, drop out

of school in each state listed on the left hand side.

Try another example. Look at the following and then decide who the graph is talking about.

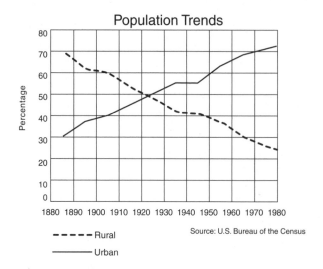

Question

1. Who is the graph talking about?

    _____

    _____

    _____

    _____

    _____

Answer

1. The graph is talking about people who live in rural and urban areas. Rural areas are outside of cities where few people live; urban areas are heavily populated cities. Anytime a chart has the word "population" in its title you know that it has to do with numbers of people. The words "rural" and "urban" at the bottom of this chart tell you what kinds of population the chart talks about. The numbers on the left hand side represent the percent of population, the numbers on the bottom of the chart represent years in history.

Now let's try a few examples using the word *what*. Read the following and answer the following question.

Educational Statistics, 1870-1910

	Total enrollment in public elementary and secondary schools	Enrollment, grades 9-12 and postgraduates (public schools)	Percentage of population 17 years old graduating from high school	Bachelors, or first professional degrees, awarded by institutions of higher education
1870	6,871,522	80,277	2.0%	9,371
1880	9,867,505	110,277	2.5%	12,896
1890	12,722,581	202,963	3.5%	15,539
1900	15,503,110	519,251	6.4%	27,410
1910	17,813,852	915,061	8.8%	37,199

Question

1. What is the table about?

_____

_____

_____

_____

_____

Answer

1. The table shows educational statistics for the years 1870–1910. The table consists of four columns, each containing a different type of educational statistic, a different educational related fact. The vertical column on the left side lists different years. The table tells you how many people were enrolled in school, how many of those were enrolled in grades 9–12, the percent of people who graduated from high school at age 17, and the number of people who obtained bachelor's degrees.

Try another example using the question *what*. Read the following chart and explain what it is talking about.

PRESIDENTIAL PREFERENCES OF DIFFERENT GROUPS

	Reagan	Carter
Total Sample	37	30
Democrats (29%)	18	56
Independents (43%)	32	24
Republicans (24%)	72	9
Detroit (15%)	24	57
Rest of tri-county area (25%)	40	28
Remainder of state (59%)	40	24
Liberal (22%)	26	37
Middle of the road (30%)	33	31
Conservative (42%)	50	25
Labor union households (37%)	30	34
Nonunion households (52%)	42	27
Black (10%)	4	73
White (87%)	41	25
Men (44%)	39	27
Women (56%)	36	32

Question

1. What is the chart about?

_____

_____

_____

_____

_____

Answer

1. The chart is about which groups of people voted for Reagan and what groups voted for Carter. The kinds of groups are listed on the left hand side, vertically (up and down).

Asking the question *where* can be helpful in understanding a chart or graph. Read the following and answer where it happened.

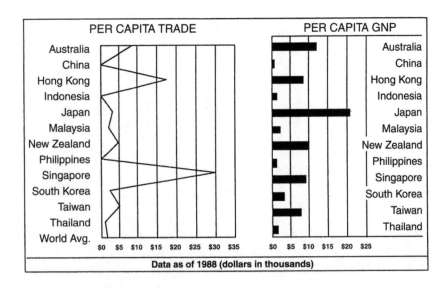

Question

1. Which three countries had the highest per capita GNP?

_____

_____

_____

Answer

1.   According to the graph, Japan, Australia, and New Zealand had the highest per capita GNP. The countries are listed vertically down the right hand side of the graph. GNP stands for gross national product. The GNP is how much total revenue a country makes, or a country's total output of goods and services, like consumer purchases.

Try another example using *where*.

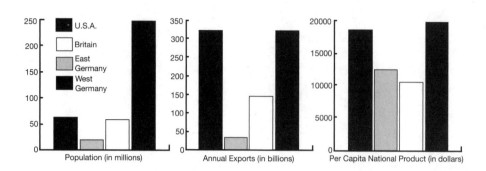

Questions

1. Where was the population greatest?

_____

2. Where were the most annual exports?

_____

3. Where was the per capita national product the greatest?

_____

Answers

1. In the United States, as shown in the first section of the graph.

2. In both West Germany and the United States, as shown in the middle section of the graph.

3. In the United States, as the last section of the graph shows.

Asking the question *when* can also be helpful when trying to read a graph or chart. Read the following graph about immigration and answer the question *when*.

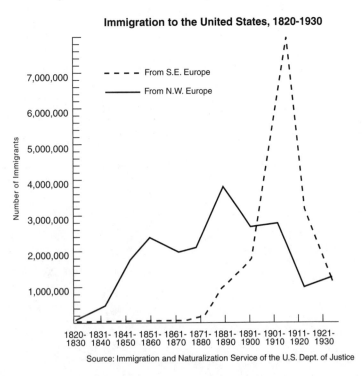

Immigration to the United States, 1820-1930

Source: Immigration and Naturalization Service of the U.S. Dept. of Justice

Question

1. This graph is about immigration to the United States. When did this immigration take place?

_____

_____

_____

_____

_____

Answer

1. From the years 1820–1930. The years are listed in 10 year intervals horizontally (across) along the bottom of the graph. The years covered are also listed in the title of the graph.

Read the chart below, and answer the question that follows.

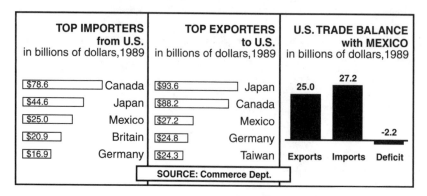

Question

1. When were the billions of dollars in U.S. goods imported and exported from the U.S.?

_____

_____

_____

_____

_____

Answer

1. In 1989, as shown in all three columns in the chart. The first column shows the value of U.S. goods imported from the U.S. The middle section shows which countries were top exporters to the U.S. and how much they exported. The last column shows the U.S. trade balance with Mexico.

REVIEW

The skills needed for approaching graphs and charts are similar to the ones we discussed in approaching reading passages. The three steps involved in reading a graph are:

- Previewing the graph

- Getting the main idea from a graph

- Interpreting data

Previewing graphs by reading over the headings and picking up on repeated data helps us get a focus on what the chart or graph is about. Getting a rough idea of what we are dealing with gives us something to focus on so we will not be confused by all the data we face.

Getting the main idea involves putting all the facts together so you can see why this chart or graph was drawn. Knowing the main idea is very important because it makes it easier in understanding all the details.

Asking yourself _who, what, where,_ and _when_ is a good way to interpret data presented by a graph or chart.

If you put these three skills together and practice them often, you will find graphs and charts easier to understand. Practice using these skills on the next page.

☞ Practice: Understanding Graphs and Charts

DIRECTIONS: Read the following passages. Apply the strategies you've learned in this chapter. Write in the margins and mark up the text as you go. Then answer the questions following each passage.

Questions 1–5 are based on the following table.

U.S. City Populations – 1988 (Selected Cities)

San Diego, California	1,070,310
Omaha, Nebraska	353,170
Baltimore, Maryland	751,400
Houston, Texas	1,698,090
Boston, Massachusetts	577,830
New York, New York	7,352,700

1. What is the main idea of the table?

    _____

    _____

2. What region of the world is the table referring to?

    _____

    _____

3. The information in this table reflects the demographics of U.S. cities from what year?

    _____

    _____

4. Do the numbers run in the thousands, hundreds of thousands, or millions?

    _____

    _____

5. Which city has the fewest people?

    _____

    _____

Questions 6–12 are based on the following chart.

New York Stock Exchange Companies with Largest Number of Stockholders, 1985	
Company	**Stockholders**
American Telephone & Telegraph (AT&T)	2,927,000
General Motors	1,990,000
Bell South Corp.	1,685,000
Bell Atlantic	1,413,000
American Information Tech.	1,382,000
NYNEX Corp.	1,348,000
Southwestern Bell	1,320,000
Pacific Telesis Group	1,242,000
US WEST	1,156,000
International Business Machines	798,000
Exxon Corp.	785,000
General Electric	490,000
GTE Corp.	442,000
Bell Canada Enterprises	332,000
Sears Roebuck	326,000

From *1986 Fact Book,* copyright New York Stock Exchange, Inc., 1986.

6. What is the title of the table?

_____

_____

7. What other words are in boldface?

_____

_____

8. What is the main idea of the table?

_____

_____

9. What are some companies listed on the table?

_____

_____

10. What company on the table had the most stockholders?

_____

_____

11. Where were these stocks listed?

_____

_____

12. When did these companies have this many shareholders?

_____

_____

Questions 13–18 are based on the following table.

Demographic Statistics of Selected States in the United States—1989

State	Population	Approximate Population Density	Land Area (Square Mile)	Per Capita Income
Virginia	6,098,000	149	37,704	$16,399
Rhode Island	998,000	823	1,055	$18,061
Massachusetts	5,913,000	713	7,824	$22,196
Georgia	6,436,000	109	58,056	$16,188
New York	17,950,000	366	47,377	$20,540

13. What is the title of the table?

    _____

    _____

14. The information in this table is from what year?

    _____

    _____

15. What states are included in this table?

    _____

    _____

16. What does "Approximate Population Density" mean?

    _____

    _____

17. Which state has the highest per capita income?

    _____

    _____

18. Does the state with the lowest per capita income also have the lowest population?

    _____

    _____

Answers

1. The main idea of the table is in its title, which is *U.S. City Populations*. The table tells us how many people live in several U.S. cities.

2. The table refers only to cities in the United States. This answer can be found in the title of the table.

3. 1988. The answer can be found in the title.

4. Some of the numbers are in the hundreds of thousands; some are in the millions. To find the answer, look at how many digits are in the numbers. For example, "577,830" has six digits (numbers) in it. That means it is "five *hundred* seventy seven *thousand* eight hundred thirty." A number such as "1,070,310" has seven digits, which means it is "one *million*, seventy thousand, three hundred ten."

5. The city of Omaha, Nebraska has the fewest people with 353,170.

6. The title is: *New York Stock Exchange Companies with Largest Number of Shareholders, 1985.*

7. The words **company** and **stockholders** are in boldface.

8. The main idea of the table is to show which companies had the most stockholders in 1985.

9. Two of the companies, for example, are General Motors and Sears Roebuck.

10. American Telephone & Telegraph (AT&T) had the most stockholders.

11. The stocks were listed on the New York Stock Exchange.

12. The companies had this many shareholders in 1985.

13. The title is *Demographic Statistics of Selected States in the United States.*

14. 1989.

15. Virginia, Rhode Island, Massachusetts, Georgia, and New York are all mentioned.

16. "Approximate Population Density" refers to how many people live in a certain amount of space.

17. Massachusetts has the highest per capita income with $22,196 a year.

18. No. The state with the smallest population is Rhode Island with 998,000 people. However, the state with the lowest per capita income is Georgia with $16,188.

Social Studies

Reading Patterns

SOCIAL STUDIES

READING PATTERNS

This chapter will further explain and demonstrate how to answer GED social studies questions based on passages. The chapter "Comprehending What You Read" offered suggestions for understanding passages and this chapter will offer help in more difficult aspects of the passages. In the first section you will learn how to compare and contrast facts in any given passage. In section two you will be shown how to identify sequences (or order) of events. In section three you will learn how to answer questions based on cause and effect relationships. Section four explains how to infer meanings in passages, an often used type of GED question. Finally, section five will show you how to distinguish fact from opinion.

COMPARING AND CONTRASTING

Comparing and contrasting will be

covered in this section. "Compare and contrast" simply means showing how things are alike (compare) and how they are different (contrast). There are usually signal words in a passage that tell you that the author is comparing and contrasting. These words are usually: also, like, as well as, however, on the other hand, although, and yet. For example, read the following sentence and decide what is being compared or contrasted. *Dogs tend to enjoy the company of humans, while cats, on the other hand, tend to like being alone.* The author thinks a difference, or contrast, between dogs and cats is that dogs like being around people, but cats would rather be alone.

Read the following paragraph. Look for the key or signal words that tell you when something is being compared or contrasted. Answer the questions that follow.

The Industrial Revolution began with inventions like the sewing machine in the mid 18th century. These inventions made it easier for products to be produced at a faster rate. The Industrial Revolution caused a shift in population. Before the revolution most people lived in rural areas, but after it many more people moved to the cities to look for work in the new factories. On the one hand, the new factories were good for people because they created more jobs. On the other hand, they were sources of hardship for people because some of the factories were dangerous, overcrowded, and produced unsanitary conditions.

Questions

1. What was being compared and contrasted in the passage?

   _____

   _____

2. What is the author's opinion about life before and after factories?

   _____

   _____

Answers

1. Life before factories was being compared to life after factories.

2. The author thinks that the factories were good because they created jobs but bad because of the conditions in which people had to work.

Here is an example about the Great Depression. Read it carefully to determine what is being compared and contrasted.

The Great Depression began in 1929 with the crash of the stock market. Banks closed, many people lost their savings, and many people lost their jobs. Franklin Roosevelt was elected in 1932. He tried many new programs to end the Depression such as the Works Progress Administration and the Civilian Conservation Corps. He encouraged Congress to pass the social security law. Although some of these programs were successful, many people feel that World War II really ended the Depression, and not FDR.

Questions

1. What is being compared and contrasted?

   _____

   _____

2. What does the author think about the success of FDR's programs?

   _____

   _____

Answers

1. What happened during the Depression before and after the election of FDR.

2. The author does not give an opinion but only states that some people think that the start of the war ended the Depression.

Here is an example based on geography and weather. First look for the main idea of the paragraph. Next, think about what you already know about the subject. Finally, look for the signal words that tell you when something is being compared and contrasted.

There are many interesting places to visit in the United States, and when planning a trip to one of them, keep in mind what the weather will be like there. For example, you might want to visit the midwest, which contains the states of North Dakota, South Dakota, Nebraska, Kansas, Minnesota, Iowa, Missouri, Wisconsin, Illinois, Michigan, Indiana, and Ohio. They can be nice places to visit. However, when planning to go there keep in mind that the region gets bitterly cold and windy in the winter. You also might want to visit the southwest, which includes states like Arizona and New Mexico. When going there keep in mind that it is extremely and even dangerously hot in the summer months.

Questions

1. What is the main idea of the passage?

_____

_____

2. What did you already know about the subject before reading the paragraph?

_____

_____

_____

3. What is one example from the passage on the previous page where something is compared and contrasted?

_____

_____

Answers

1. The main idea, in this case, is the first sentence.

2. Perhaps you have watched the news and have noticed what the weather is like around the country.

3. The midwest tends to be cold while the southwest tends to be hot.

Here is an example about Canada. Read the passage to decipher what is being compared and contrasted.

Canada is the country that lies to the north of the United States and is also on the continent of North America. The capital of Canada is Ottawa. The United States and Canada are alike in several ways. People in both countries speak English and have similar economic bases and cultures. Canada, however, has a population of over 29

million people. The United States has a population of over 280 million people.

Questions

1. What is being compared in the above passage?

_____

_____

2. How are the United States and Canada similar?

_____

_____

3. How are the two countries different?

_____

_____

Answers

1. The United States and Canada are being compared in the passage.

2. People in both countries speak English. They have similar economic situations and cultures.

3. The populations of Canada and the United States are different; Canada's population is much smaller.

Here is another example to use to practice comparing and contrasting. This passage is based on behavioral science.

Here is an example based on a famous U.S. Supreme Court case. This case made it illegal for a police officer to arrest suspects without first telling them of their right to a lawyer and telling them that they do not have to speak until they have an attorney.

Miranda's case reached the U.S. Supreme Court in 1966. It was certainly a difficult case. On the one hand, there was the important question of the rights of a person under the protection of the Constitution. On the other hand, there was the equally important issue of interfering with the work of the police.

Question

1. What is being compared and contrasted?

_____

_____

Answer

1. The rights of a person being arrested are compared and contrasted with the rights of the police to do their job.

IDENTIFYING SEQUENCES

In this section you will learn to recognize the sequence, or order, of events in any given passage. Sometimes the order of events is given by stating what happened first, what happened second, and so on. Other times, the author gives dates that tell you the order in which things happen. Other times, the author only gives clues like the words *next*, *finally*, and *later*. We will begin with the simpler examples and move on to the more difficult examples.

Read the following paragraph. Look for clues that tell you the sequence of events.

What became known as the Watergate crisis began during the 1972 presidential campaign. First, on June 17, a security officer for the Committee for the Re-election of the President, and four others broke into Democratic headquarters at the Watergate apartments and were caught. They

Photo courtesy of Richard Milhous Nixon Materials Project

President Nixon departing after resigning August 9, 1973.

had been trying to install eavesdropping machines. Second, the trial of the burglars began in 1973. Third, Nixon refused to allow an investigation committee to go through White House documents in order to investigate who was involved. Lastly, Nixon resigned knowing that there was a possibility he would be impeached.

Questions

1. What event occurred first?

   _____

   _____

2. What happened second?

   _____

   _____

3. What happened third?

   _____

   _____

4. What happened fourth and last?

   _____

   _____

Answers

1. Several men broke into Democratic headquarters. This occurred on June 17, 1972.

2. The trial of the burglars began in 1973.

3. Nixon refused to allow White House documents to be searched.

4. Nixon resigned knowing that there was a possibility he would be impeached.

Try another example. Read the following and then answer the questions that accompany it.

When the English first came to America they settled in Virginia. They named the area for their sovereign Queen Elizabeth I, who was known as the "virgin queen." Life was very difficult in Virginia. The mortality rate was very high, primarily due to contagious diseases. The second place they settled was called Plymouth. The Plymouth colony was settled by Puritans. The colony was eventually absorbed into the larger colony called Massachusetts Bay. The third colony to be founded was called Maryland. This colony was founded by a Catholic man named Lord Baltimore. His colony underwent extreme political disorder, due to the tensions between Catholics and Protestants.

Questions

1. What event happened first?

   _____

   _____

2. What event happened second?

   _____

3. What event happened third?

   _____

   _____

Answers

1. Virginia was settled by the English. It is stated that when the English first came to America, they settled in Virginia.

2.   Plymouth was settled by the Puritans. It is stated that the second place they settled was called Plymouth.

3.   The colony of Maryland was settled. It is stated that the third colony to be founded was called Maryland.

Now try a couple of examples that use dates, instead of clue words, to identify the sequence of events.

In 1941 Japan bombed the U.S. ships in Pearl Harbor, Hawaii and forced American entry into World War II. In 1945, the U.S. Navy sailed into Tokyo Bay and forced its will on a defeated Japan.

Questions

1.   What event happened first?

_____

_____

2.   What happened second?

_____

_____

Answers

1.   Japan bombed Pearl Harbor. This occurred in 1941. The U.S. Navy sailed into Tokyo Bay in 1945, four years later. Japan bombed Pearl Harbor first.

2.   The U.S. Navy sailed into Tokyo Bay. This occurred in 1945. Japan bombed Pearl Harbor in 1941, four years earlier. The U.S. Navy sailed into Tokyo Bay second.

Try another example. Read the passage and find the main idea. Then identify the sequence of events.

There are two major ways in which the federal government protects Americans from problems in the banking industry. They are contained in the Federal Reserve System and the Federal Deposit Insurance Corporation. The Federal Reserve System was established in 1913. It regulates the banking industry. All banks must be members of the Federal Reserve System. The Federal Deposit Insurance Corporation (FDIC) was established in 1933. The FDIC insures people's money. Each person is insured for up to $100,000.

Questions

1.   What is the main idea of the paragraph?

_____

_____

2.   What happened first?

_____

_____

3.   What happened second?

_____

_____

Answers

1.   The first sentence encompasses the main idea. It reads, *There are two major ways in which the federal government protects Americans from problems in the banking industry.*

2.   The Federal Reserve System was created. It was established in 1913. The FDIC was not established until 1933.

3. The FDIC was created. It occurred after the Federal Reserve System was created.

Now let's try some examples using clue words like *next*, *last*, and *finally*. Read the following and answer the questions that accompany it.

Hitler was appointed Chancellor of Germany in 1933. He then quickly destroyed the government of the Weimar Republic. Next, he established mass organizations such as the Nazi Labor Front and Hitler Youth. He then started the mass persecution of Jews. Jewish property was destroyed, many Jews were sent to live in Jewish ghettos, and many were murdered. Finally, Hitler achieved total control over Germany's armed forces in 1937 and 1938.

Questions

1. Did Hitler establish the Hitler Youth before or after 1933?

   _____

   _____

2. What happened last?

   _____

   _____

3. Between what years did the persecution of Jews start?

   _____

   _____

Answers

1. Hitler established the Hitler Youth after 1933. The text says that he was appointed Chancellor in 1933 and later established Hitler Youth.

2. Hitler achieved control over the armed forces. This occurred in 1937 and 1938.

3. The persecution of the Jews started between 1933 and 1937. These are the only dates given and we know that it was after 1933, when Hitler became Chancellor, and before 1937, when he achieved control over the armed forces.

Try another example. Read the following paragraph and answer the questions that accompany it.

Italian unification was first attempted in 1848. Before the attempts at unification, the modern country of Italy was actually several states, some of which were controlled by the Austrian empire. The 1848 attempt was stopped by the Austrians. Next, Camillo Cavour became one of the leaders of the unification movement. He believed that a future united Italy could only occur if it was governed by Italians themselves, not by Austrians. Finally, Italian unification was realized in 1870.

Questions

1. Who controlled part of Italy before 1870?

   _____

   _____

2. Did Cavour become a unification leader before or after Italian unification was realized?

   _____

   _____

Answers

1. The Austrians controlled part of Italy before 1870.

2.   Camillo Cavour became a unification leader before Italian unification was realized in 1870.

Try another example. The following is from a speech. It is about slavery. All of the people mentioned in the excerpt were slaves who rebelled against slavery and won their freedom. Look for the main idea first, and then identify the sequence of events.

In 1822, Denmark Vesey of South Carolina formed a plan for the liberation of his fellowmen (fellow slaves). The patriotic Nathaniel Turner followed Denmark Vesey. Next arose the immortal Joseph Cinque, the hero of the Amistad. Next arose Madison Washington, that bright star of freedom. Nineteen struck for liberty or death. Only one life was taken, and the whole party were emancipated.

Questions

1.   What is the main idea of the paragraph?

_____

_____

2.   Who arose first: Nat Turner or Madison Washington?

_____

_____

3.   If you were to add the word "finally" to the paragraph, where would you put it?

_____

_____

Answers

1.   The main idea of the paragraph is a plan for the liberation of slaves that Denmark Vesey formed. This can be found in the first sentence.

2.   Nat Turner arose before Madison. Madison Washington arose after Nat Turner, Denmark Vesey, and Joseph Cinque.

3.   Before the last sentence, directly before the word "only."

CAUSE AND EFFECT RELATIONSHIPS

In this section you will learn how to identify cause and effect relationships. The "cause" is why something happened. The "effect" is what happened because of the cause. For example, read this sentence: Mary broke her leg when she fell off the roof. What caused her leg to break was falling off the roof; the effect was breaking her leg. In this section you will have the opportunity to read many passages that deal with social studies and have cause and effect relationships.

Read the following passage carefully and answer the questions that accompany it.

Fascism is an ideology that developed in the late 19th and early 20th centuries. It developed as a reaction to what people perceived as a failure of democratic governments to fix the social and economic problems of the period. In the fascists' model the state's interests are more important than individual desires and rights. National pride and patriotism are more than demonstrations of civic responsibility, they are essential parts of being a citizen. Each individual must comply with the regulations that have been established by the state. They cannot question those regulations.

Questions

1. According to the passage, what was the cause of fascism?

   _____

   _____

2. What is the effect that accompanies question #1?

   _____

   _____

Answers

1. Fascism was caused by a reaction to the perceived failure of democracy.

2. The creation of fascism is the effect of people's perceived failure of democracy.

Let's try another example on European history that deals with cause and effect relationships. This time there will also be a question regarding a word that you might not know.

The Marshall Plan was designed in 1947 by George C. Marshall, who was secretary of state under President Truman. Marshall created the plan because he was concerned that if the European countries did not recover economically from the war then they might be subject to communist ideology. The Marshall Plan, also called the European Recovery Plan, was an aid program wherein the U.S. would loan Western European countries and others money. The plan was highly successful, and it greatly helped the economies of France, Italy, and Great Britain, among others.

Questions

1. Name one cause listed in the passage.

   _____

   _____

2. What effect accompanies that cause?

   _____

   _____

3. Name another cause/effect relationship from the passage.

   _____

   _____

4. What does the word "ideology" mean?

   _____

   _____

Answers

1.   The Marshall Plan was caused by the fear of countries falling to communism.

2.   If the cause is fear of communism then the effect is the Marshall Plan.

3.   The Marshall Plan caused economic recovery in some European countries and they did not fall to communism. The economic recovery would be the effect.

4.   It means, in this case, the communist way of thinking, or the communist philosophy.

Try another example based on European history. Look for the cause and effect relationship in the passage. You will also be asked for the definition of a word that you might not know.

Europe's scientific revolution, which occurred between the years 1500 and 1700, revolutionized human thinking. The new science brought forth the idea that humans could understand the operation of the physical world through the use of their reason. Copernicus was one person who influenced this new thinking. He rejected the view that the planet Earth was at the center of the universe and put forth the idea that the sun was at the center. Isaac Newton, another scientist from this period, discovered the laws of motion, gravity, and inertia.

Questions

1.   What caused the human way of thinking to change?

_____

_____

2.   Who were two scientists that caused the scientific revolution?

_____

_____

3.   What does the word "revolutionize" mean?

_____

_____

Answers

1.   The scientific revolution caused the human way of thinking to change. It states in the message that Europe's scientific revolution, which occurred between the years 1500 and 1700, revolutionized human thinking.

2.   Copernicus and Newton caused the scientific revolution. Copernicus rejected the view that the planet Earth was at the center of the universe and put forth the idea that the sun was at the center. Newton discovered the laws of motion, gravity, and inertia.

3.   It means to change drastically. In this context, this can be figured out by thinking about the word "revolution." The scientific revolution brought about a new way of thinking, so it changed the old way of thinking. If something revolutionizes something else, it brings about a new way of doing things.

Read the following passage based on U.S. history. Look for cause and effect relationships.

The Ku Klux Klan was created during America's Reconstruction era. Reconstruction was the period after the Civil War when the Southern states were responding politically to losing the war and having terrible economic difficulties. The Northerners attempted to reconstruct the

South so that blacks and whites had more equal rights. Some Southerners, wanting to return life to the way it had been before the war, responded to this by creating the KKK. This organization aimed violent tactics at blacks and white Republicans and intimidated many people out of voting.

Questions

1. What caused some Southerners to create the KKK?

   _____

   _____

2. What was the effect of the Southerners creating the KKK?

   _____

   _____

Answers

1. Some Southerners, wanting to return to the way of life they had before the Civil War, responded to this by creating the KKK.

2. The KKK used violent tactics, aimed at black and white Republicans, to intimidate them from voting.

Here is another example. This time, first look for the main idea. Then look for at least one supporting idea. Next, look for cause and effect relationships. The word "coup" loosely means "overthrow" or "sudden action."

During the American Revolutionary War a military coup was diverted by Washington himself. The Continental army was poorly paid, when they were paid at all. When the war was almost over, the army was waiting for results of peace negotiations. Fears spread among the soldiers that the army might be disbanded without pay

or pension. Only a personal appeal by Washington to his soldiers prevented the situation from exploding into a military crisis and a military coup.

Questions

1. What is the main idea of the passage?

   _____

   _____

2. What is one supporting sentence?

   _____

   _____

3. What almost caused a military crisis or coup?

   _____

   _____

4. What was the effect of Washington's personal appeal to the soldiers?

   _____

   _____

Answers

1. In this case, the main idea is the first sentence of the passage. It reads, *During the American Revolutionary War, a military coup was diverted by Washington himself.*

2. "Fears spread among the soldiers that the army might be disbanded without pay or pension."

3. Fears among the soldiers that they might not be paid or receive a pension almost caused a military crisis or coup.

4. They did not attempt a coup or cause a crisis.

Here is another example. Look for cause/effect relationships. You will also be asked to define words that you might not know.

The Bay of Pigs affair was a humiliating embarrassment for President Kennedy. The affair was the attempt to oust Castro in Cuba. Kennedy, after he had been in office for only two months, decided to go ahead with a project that would use Cuban exiles to start an anti-Castro rebellion in Cuba and oust Castro. The Cuban exiles were ferried ashore at the Bay of Pigs in Cuba with American support and equipment, but when they got there, the Cuban people did not rise up in revolt. After two days of being trapped by the Cuban military, the U.S. forces rescued the surviving 20% of the Bay of Pigs invasion force.

Questions

1. Why was the Bay of Pigs invasion an embarrassment for Kennedy?

   _____

   _____

2. What caused President Kennedy to want to invade Cuba?

   _____

   _____

3. What was the effect of the Cuban people not uprising in revolt?

   _____

   _____

4. What does the word "oust" mean?

   _____

   _____

5. What does the word "inherited" mean?

   _____

   _____

Answers

1. The invasion was an embarrassment for President Kennedy because it was a failure.

2. He wanted to overthrow Castro and his communist regime.

3. The effect was the invasion failed. The invasion plans depended on the Cuban people helping the exiles to overthrow Castro.

4. "Oust" means to overthrow or get rid of. In this case, Kennedy wanted to overthrow Castro as leader of Cuba.

5. It means that something was passed down. In this case, the Bay of Pigs idea was passed down to Kennedy after Eisenhower left office.

Here is another example based on a U.S. history passage. Find the main idea and then look for cause and effect relationships.

The Knights of Labor was an American labor union. It was founded in 1869 by workers in Philadelphia's garment district. They were the only major union of their time to extend membership to blacks, women, and unskilled workers. They wanted a society where employees and employers would work together. Following a series of failed strikes ending in the disastrous Haymarket Square riot in 1886, the group began to break up into smaller crafts unions and other more radical groups. They were eventually replaced by the AFL in the 1890s as America's major labor union.

Questions

1. What is the main idea of the passage?

_____

_____

2. What caused the Knights of Labor to break into smaller unions?

_____

_____

Answers

1. The first sentence is the main idea; it reads, *The Knights of Labor was an American labor union.*

2. A series of failed strikes that ended in the disastrous Haymarket Square riot caused the Knights of Labor to break into smaller unions.

INFERRING MEANING

In this section you will learn how to infer meanings from a passage. Sometimes you must figure out what the author is saying when he or she is not obviously stating it. When you do that it is called inferring the meaning. For example, read the following sentence. "When people camp out they sometimes run into bears, most of which do not hurt them." In that sentence, the author clearly and obviously states that most bears do not hurt campers. You can *infer* that the author is also saying that, occasionally, bears do hurt campers. In this section you will have several opportunities to try to infer meanings from passages.

Here is an example based on a passage that you have already seen in this book. Look for the inferred meanings.

There are two major ways in which the federal government protects Americans from problems in the banking industry. The Federal Reserve System was established in 1913. It regulates the banking industry. The Federal Deposit Insurance Corporation was established in 1933. The FDIC insures people's money. Each person is insured for up to $100,000.

Question

1. A reader can infer a meaning about what the author says about the FDIC. What is it?

_____

_____

Answer

1. That each person's money *in a bank* is insured for up to $100,000, depending on how much they had in their account. You can infer this by looking closely at what the author says.

He says in the main sentence that the paragraph will be about the banking industry. Then he talks about people's money being insured by the government. From this you can infer that the money being insured is not under someone's mattress, but in a bank.

Here is another example. Look for the inferred meanings.

> Hoover had been in office less than a year, and stocks had been falling for over a month. Business was still good; almost everyone thought a rally must be close at hand. The market opened steady with prices little changed from the previous day. It sagged easily for the first half hour, and then around eleven o'clock the deluge broke.

Question

1. What should you infer about the event that takes place in the paragraph?

   _____

   _____

Answer

1. You can infer that the author is talking about the stock market crash. The author never puts the title "stock market" together, so that is why you have to infer it. She does, however, mention stocks falling and the market opening steady.

Try this example. It is also from a passage that you have already seen in this book. Look first for the main idea and then look for the inferred meanings.

> Fascism is an ideology that developed in the late 19th century and early 20th century. It developed as a reaction to what people perceived as a failure of

democratic governments to fix the social and economic problems of the period. In the fascists' model the state's interests are more important than individual desires and rights. National pride and patriotism are more than demonstrations of civic responsibility; they are essential parts of being a citizen.

Questions

1. What is the main idea?

   _____

   _____

2. What can you infer in the first two sentences about fascists?

   _____

   _____

3. Remembering that fascism was a reaction to democracy, what can you infer from the third sentence of the passage?

   _____

   _____

Answers

1. In this case, it is the first sentence. It says, *Fascism is an ideology that developed in the late 19th century and early 20th century.*

2. You can infer that fascism is not democratic, as fascists developed their theories based on thinking that democracy does not work for them. You can also infer that the people who perceived democracy to be a failure are the ones who became fascists.

3. You can infer that in a democratic model, the individual's rights are more important than the state's interests.

Here is one last example that you have already seen. The subsequent passages will be new.

The Ku Klux Klan was created during America's Reconstruction era. Reconstruction was the period after the Civil War when the Southern states were responding politically to losing the war and having terrible economic difficulties. The Northerners attempted to reconstruct the South so that blacks and whites had more equal rights. Some Southerners, wanting to return life to the way it had been before the war, responded to this by creating the KKK. This organization aimed violent tactics at blacks and white Republicans and intimidated many people out of voting.

Question

1. The paragraph says that white Republicans were targeted by members of the KKK. What can you infer from this about the position of white Republicans?

_____

_____

Answer

1. They were anti-KKK and wanted the blacks to have equal rights.

Try the following example. The passage is based on the U.S. government. Look for inferred meanings.

Nine of the thirteen states had to approve of the Constitution for it to become the law of the land. A battle ensued between those favoring the plan, the Federalists, and those opposing it, the Anti-Federalists. The disputed issues involved the increased power of the central government at the expense of the states and the lack of a bill of rights guaranteeing individual pro-

tections to the citizens. Pro-Constitution leaders James Madison, John Jay, and Alexander Hamilton published a series of articles to persuade people to support the Constitution. The papers were known as *The Federalist*.

Questions

1. What do you need to infer about the word "battle" in order to understand the paragraph?

_____

_____

2. What do you need to infer about the position of Madison, Jay, and Hamilton?

_____

_____

Answers

1. The word "battle," in this case, means a battle of words and emotions, not one of weapons and killing.

2. Although it is never stated, they were Federalists. The author does state that they were supporters of the Constitution and wrote papers called *The Federalist*.

Here is an example that is, again, based on the U.S. government. Find the main idea and then find inferred meanings.

The legislative process is time-consuming. A bill can be introduced in either house where it is referred to the appropriate committee. Next, the bill goes to a subcommittee that will schedule a hearing if the members think that it is worthy of one. A bill originating in the House must pass through the Rules Committee before going on to the full House. If the bill passes in the full chamber, it is then sent on to the other chamber to begin the process all over again. Most of the thousands of bills introduced in Congress die in committee with less than five percent becoming law.

Questions

1. What is the main idea?

_____

_____

2. What can be inferred about the difference between a bill going before the "appropriate committee" and a bill going before the full house?

_____

_____

Answers

1. That the legislative process is time-consuming, as stated in the first sentence.

2. The full house refers to either all of the Senate or all of the House of Representatives. The "appropriate committee" only represents a section of the full Senate or full House of Representatives.

Here is a passage about the term "gender gap." Read it and answer the questions that follow.

The term gender gap refers to the fact that women and men have different views on some political topics. According to a poll taken in 1990, women support gun control by 85%, compared to men's 72%. Women support more spending for social security by 60% to men's 50%. Women also support less military spending by 40% compared to men's 49%.

Questions

1. What should you infer about what the other 15% of women polled in 1990 preferred in regard to gun control?

_____

_____

2. What can be inferred about the percent of men polled in 1990 that wanted the government to spend the same amount or more on the military?

_____

_____

3. What could be inferred about women's support of spending more on Medicare and Medicaid?

_____

_____

Answers

1. You should infer that 15% of women polled in 1990 did not support gun control. You should infer that because 85% of women *support* gun control.

2. You can infer that 51% wanted the same or more spent on the military. You can infer this because 49% supported less military spending.

3. It could be inferred that women would support spending more on those programs. This could be inferred because 85% of women polled wanted more spending on social security and most people, but not all, who would support that would also support Medicare.

DISTINGUISHING FACT FROM OPINION

In this section you will learn how to tell the difference between a fact and an opinion. In some passages this difference is hard to see. The difference between a fact and an opinion is that a fact can be proved, it is either true or it is not. An opinion is something that a person only thinks is true.

Read the following paragraph. Distinguish fact from opinion.

History is a discipline that can be studied, interpreted, and taught in many different ways. For example, some historians think that it should be studied and taught from the point of view of the masses, or the common people. This is usually referred to as "social history." Others think that history is best understood by looking at the points of view of those in power, while others still look at the economics of a time period as the definitive aspect of history.

Question

1. Is it a fact or an opinion that social history is the best way to understand history?

   _____

   _____

Answer

1. It is an opinion. The answer can be found in key phrases such as "some historians think" and "others think." Such a use of the word "think" tells us that an opinion is about to be stated, and not a fact. Also, the first sentence says that history can be studied, interpreted, and taught in many different ways, which implies that there are many opinions regarding the best way to approach it.

Read the following and then answer the questions that accompany it.

On February 9, 1950, Senator Joseph McCarthy of Wisconsin stated that he had a list of known communists who were working in the State Department. What followed was a wave of attacks on diplomats and members of the U.S. government that lasted until he was censured by the Senate in 1954. There are many theories to explain why McCarthy succeeded in obtaining support for his accusations and attacks. Some people believe that the end of the Second World War brought new fears, as the fear of a nuclear war became a reality. This new fear made people want to secure their communities against any communist threat. Others believe that McCarthy and his supporters' motive was purely political. They simply wanted to discredit President Truman's Fair Deal.

Questions

1. Is it a fact or an opinion that McCarthy was a senator from Wisconsin?

   _____

   _____

2. Does the paragraph offer any facts to support why McCarthy had followers?

   _____

   _____

Answers

1. It is a fact. This can be proved. It is true.

2. No, it only offers the opinions of some people. The phrase "some people believe" tells you that an opinion is about to be stated.

Here is one last example. Find the facts and the opinions.

> Many school districts are trying out new ways to teach immigrant children English. One type of school simply puts children in a class with other children their age, regardless of the fact that the child does not understand the language. The child is also given special tutoring during the day so that they can learn the language. This is called mainstreaming because the child is being pushed into the normal mainstream, or regular school classroom. Another type of program is one where immigrant children are instructed in their native language so that they will learn the concepts being taught, like facts in history or addition. They are also given English lessons. Another type of school program tries to put the children who do not speak English into a regular classroom, but gives them special teachers in that room to translate and help them when needed throughout the day.

Questions

1. If the author closed the paragraph by saying that she believes that the third method is the best, would that be fact or opinion?

    _____

    _____

2. Are there any opinions offered in the passage?

    _____

    _____

Answers

1. It would be an opinion. The author would *think* that is true.

2. No, there are no opinions offered. The passage only offers facts that can be verified. If a fact can be verified that means that one could check by asking school districts if they have tried these methods. If they have, then the facts are verified and are true.

REVIEW

In this chapter we covered the following methods of approaching topics in social studies:

*   Comparing and Contrasting

*   Identifying Sequences

*   Cause and Effect Relationships

*   Inferring Meaning

*   Distinguishing Fact from Opinion

Comparing and contrasting is analytical practice that helps us because it makes us prepare a mental list of what makes two things similar and what makes them different. By doing this we not only see the relationship between two things but we also learn more about each of the places, events, or people we are comparing because we find out what makes them so unique.

Identifying sequences is important in social studies because it is critical to understand when certain events took place. If we are not able to do this, we will not be able to understand any other relationship between two events because we will not have an accurate basis from which to work.

Cause and effect relationships will always help us understand social studies and will also make it more interesting. Instead of looking at history as a list of facts and events we learn to trace the events and see how one event led to another. In economics we can follow trends and learn to anticipate certain things happening because of one particular occurrence.

Inferring meaning is important as well because many times what the author of a passage is trying to get across isn't stated directly in the passage. If we do not learn how to infer we will not fully comprehend what we have read.

A tool that works hand in hand with inferring meaning is distinguishing fact from opinion. Knowing what is a fact and what is an opinion is important whenever we are reading. It becomes a useful tool to practice in everyday life because many times we can become confused and accept as fact something that may not be true at all. When we do this we develop ideas in our heads that are false and will affect all our future ideas about the world in a negative way.

Now practice these skills on the following questions.

☞ **Practice: Reading Patterns**

DIRECTIONS: Read the following passages. Apply the strategies you've learned in this chapter. Write in the margins and mark up the text as you go. Then answer the questions following each passage.

Questions 1 and 2 refer to the following passage.

The term "Balkan states" refers to several countries in the Balkan Peninsula in Europe. The countries referred to as Balkan states include Albania, Bulgaria, Croatia, Romania, Yugoslavia, and four others.

The term "Baltic states" refers to an entirely different region of Europe. The Baltic states are located near the Baltic Sea in Northern Europe. The three Baltic states are Estonia, Latvia, and Lithuania.

1. What is being compared and contrasted?

_____

_____

2. Turkey is a part of the Balkan Peninsula. Is Turkey a Baltic state or a Balkan state?

_____

_____

Questions 3–6 refer to the following passage.

Hoover had been in office for several months and stocks had been falling for over one month. Business was still good; almost everyone thought a rally must be close at hand. The market opened steady with prices little changed from the previous day. It sagged easily for the first half hour, and then around eleven o'clock the deluge broke. The bottom simply fell out of the market. Within a few moments the ticker service was hopelessly swamped and from then on no one knew what was really happening. By 1:30 the ticker tape was nearly two hours late; by 2:30 it was 147 minutes late. The last quotation was not printed on the tape until 7:08 p.m., four hours after the close. In the meantime, Wall Street had lived through an incredible nightmare.

3. What happened first, Hoover's taking office or stock prices falling?

_____

_____

4. Did the bottom fall out of the market before or after 10:30 a.m.?

_____

_____

5. Did the ticker service become hopelessly swamped before or after 2:30?

_____

_____

6. Did Wall Street live through an incredible nightmare before or after 7:08 p.m.?

_____

_____

Questions 7 and 8 refer to the following passage.

The Indian Reorganization Act was a reversal of earlier acts that had greatly endangered the American Indians' way of life. The Act, which was approved in 1934, sought to disallow Indian lands to be broken up and sold. When these lands were divided up and sold, it broke up tribal reservations and allowed whites to move in and exploit Indian lands. Indians were also provided funds so they could purchase new land and gain control of land that had already been sold off. The Act also ended restrictions on the rights of Indians to practice tribal religions.

7. What was the effect of the dividing of Indian lands on the Indians?

_____

_____

8. What does the word "disallow" mean?

_____

_____

Questions 9 and 10 refer to the following passage.

A federal grand jury is a group of people that decide whether or not someone should be charged with a crime. This type of jury does not decide whether or not someone is guilty of a crime, only if they should stand trial for what they have been accused of. Although members of the federal grand jury can be asked to "sit" or be part of the jury for up to 36 months, they do not meet every day of the work week.

9. What can be inferred about juries that are not "grand juries"?

_____

_____

10. Do grand jury members have to miss work five days a week?

_____

_____

Questions 11–12 refer to the following passage.

The "black codes" in the South were designed to limit the rights of free blacks so that they would move North. The codes ranged from bans on assembly (coming together in groups to discuss an issue) to laws forbidding blacks to learn how to read or write. By forcing out freed blacks, the Southern whites hoped to remove role models for the enslaved blacks. There was also a fear that the free blacks would help the enslaved ones to escape or revolt. The codes were only partially successful; only some free blacks moved north. The codes just stirred up resentment regarding slavery.

11. Was it a fact or an opinion that free blacks would help enslaved blacks to revolt?

_____

_____

12. Is the author's last sentence a fact or an opinion?

_____

_____

Questions 13–16 refer to the following passage.

"Reaganomics" was the term coined for President Ronald Reagan's supply-side economic policy. Reagan believed that the way to repair the shattered economy he inherited from President Carter's term was to cut spending on domestic programs and also cut taxes for wealthy individuals and corporations. Reagan believed that the money the wealthy and the corporations kept by paying less taxes would be spent on investments and the creation of new jobs. This was also called the "trickle-down" theory because Reagan hoped that the money would trickle down to the middle class and poor.

13. What is the main idea of the passage?

_____

_____

14. When the word "believed" is used, like in the second and third sentences of the paragraph, is the author stating fact or opinion?

_____

_____

15. What facts or opinions are asserted in the last sentence?

_____

_____

16. What can be inferred by the fact that Reagan wanted to cut taxes on the wealthy and corporations, and that he also cut domestic spending?

_____

_____

Answers

1. The regions known as the "Balkan states" and "Baltic states" are being compared and contrasted.

2. The "Balkans" includes the country of Turkey. All three Baltic states are named; Turkey is not one of them. Only some of the Balkan states are named, and the phrase "four others" is written in place of the others. It can be inferred that since Turkey is a part of the Balkan Peninsula, Turkey would have to be one of those unnamed four.

3. The stock prices fell first.

4. After 10:30 a.m., in fact, after 11 a.m.

5. Before 2:30.

6. Before 7:08 p.m. The words "in the meantime" offer a clue that says that Wall Street lived through a nightmare before 7:08 p.m.

7. It broke up tribal reservations and allowed Indian lands to be exploited.

8. It means to not allow, or to make illegal.

9. They decide whether or not someone is guilty of a crime, not just whether or not that person should be charged with a crime.

10. No, the last sentence of the passage states that they do not meet every day of the week.

11. Opinion. The words "hoped to remove" clue you in to the *fact* that this was only an *opinion*.

12. Opinion. It is difficult to prove something like "resentment." In most cases a statement like this is opinion unless the author has gone to extraordinary measures to prove his statement. The word "just" also tells you that this is opinion. It is even more difficult to prove that the black codes "just" stirred up resentment.

13. The main idea is encompassed in the first sentence. It says, *"Reaganomics" was the term coined for President Ronald Reagan's supply-side economic policy.*

14. The author is stating the fact that Reagan believed in his theories. Reagan's theories themselves are opinions. He believed that supply-side economics would work, but it was only his opinion that it would.

15. The phrase that says "this is called the 'trickle-down' theory" is fact. It is also fact that Reagan hoped that the money would pass down to the middle class and poor.

16. It can be inferred that he needed to cut domestic spending because some of the tax money that he was cutting would have paid for those domestic programs.

Social Studies

Applying Information

SOCIAL STUDIES

APPLYING INFORMATION

This chapter covers how to take information from charts, graphs, maps, and political cartoons in order to answer questions on the GED. This chapter is called "Applying Information" because it is sometimes necessary to interpret and apply information that is in a graph, map, cartoon, or practical document in order to use its information in more advanced ways.

APPLYING INFORMATION FROM CHARTS

In this section you will learn how to apply information from charts in order to answer questions on the GED.

Look carefully at the chart that follows based on 1940 U.S. statistics. Answer the accompanying questions.

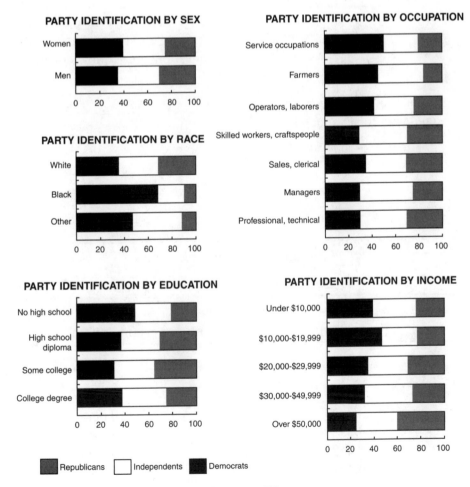

PARTY IDENTIFICATION BY SEX

PARTY IDENTIFICATION BY RACE

PARTY IDENTIFICATION BY EDUCATION

PARTY IDENTIFICATION BY OCCUPATION

PARTY IDENTIFICATION BY INCOME

Republicans ☐ Independents Democrats

From Janda, Berry, Goldman, *The Challenge of Democracy*, p. 286.

Questions

1. What does the darkest color stand for?

    _____

    _____

2. Applying the information from the chart, who would be more likely to vote for a Democratic candidate, a skilled worker or a person employed in a service occupation?

    _____

    _____

3. Who would be most likely to vote for a Republican candidate?

    _____

    _____

Answers

1. The darkest color stands for people who identified or belonged with the Democrats.

2. Applying the information from the chart, someone employed in a service occupation. You know this because in the section that shows the party preference of people in the service jobs, the darkest bar is the longest one and goes to the 45% or 50% mark. The section that shows the party preference for skilled workers and craftspeople only has the darkest bar extending to the 25% mark.

3. It looks like a tie between three occupations: skilled workers, people in sales or clerical jobs, and professional or technical people. You can tell this by looking at the gray bar on the right. The sections where the gray bar is filled up the most represent people who prefer the Republican party.

Read the chart below. The chart shows statistics for two political parties in France. You do not need to know the platform of the parties, or anything else about them, in order to answer the questions that follow correctly.

| **French Legislative Elections** | | | | |
| **Socialists** | | | **Gaullists** | |
Year	# of voters (in 1,000s)	# of seats in Parliament	# of voters (in 1,000s)	# of seats in Parliament
1958	3,176	40	4,011	196
1962	2,319	65	6,581	256
1967	4,224	117	8,449	233
1968	3,660	57	9,664	349
1973	4,523	102	8,243	270
1978	6,413	113	6,330	154
1981	9,432	270	5,231	83

Questions

1. What years does the chart span?

_____

_____

2. Applying information from the chart, when did the Socialists gain more seats in Parliament, in 1958 or in 1968?

_____

_____

3. In what year did the Gaullists have fewer voters than the Socialists?

_____

_____

4. What year did the Gaullists have fewer seats in Parliament?

_____

_____

Answers

1. The chart goes from 1958 until 1981. The years are listed in the first left column.

2. The Socialists won more seats in 1968. If you need help finding this information, look at the heading that says "Socialists." There are two columns there, one that says "# of voters" and another that says "# of seats in Parliament." Look at the second column and go one down: that is the number of seats for the year 1958. Go down three more and that is the number for the year 1968. Compare the two. The highest number is the answer.

3. The Gaullists had fewer voters than Socialists in the years 1978 and 1981. Compare the column that says "# of voters" in the Socialist category and in the Gaullist category.

4. The Gaullists had fewer seats in Parliament in 1981. Compare the second columns to each other to find the answer.

Comparison of Population in Selected Cities in the United States—1988			
City	**Population**	**City**	**Population**
New York	7,352,700	Houston	1,698,090
Los Angeles	3,352,710	Philadelphia	1,647,000
Chicago	2,977,520	San Diego	1,070,310

Demographic Statistics of Selected States in the United States—1989

State	Population	Approx. Pop. Density	Land Area Sq. Mi.	Per Capita Income
Virginia	6,098,000	149	39,704	$16,399
Rhode Island	998,000	823	1,055	$18,061
Massachusetts	5,913,000	713	7,824	$22,196
Georgia	6,436,000	109	58,056	$16,188
New York	17,950,000	366	47,377	$20,540

Read the chart on the previous page and answer the questions below.

Questions

1. What do the abbreviations in the middle column stand for?

    _____

    _____

2. What is New York's per capita income?

    _____

    _____

3. Applying information from the chart, which state has the smallest population?

    _____

    _____

4. Which state has the most land area and the least per capita income, at the same time?

    _____

    _____

5. If per capita income helps measure how well people live in a state, which state would most people pick to live in?

    _____

    _____

Answers

1. They stand for "approximate population density." Even if you do not know what this means, you can still answer questions about it correctly.

2. New York's per capita income is $20,540. Per capita income is listed in the last right column.

3. Rhode Island. To find the answer look at the column labeled "population."

4. Georgia. To find the answer look at the columns labeled land area and per capita income.

5. Massachusetts. To find the answer, look at the column labeled per capita income.

APPLYING INFORMATION FROM GRAPHS

In this section, like in the first section, you will learn how to take information from a graph and apply it to questions you are asked. Look closely at the chart on the following page and answer the questions that follow.

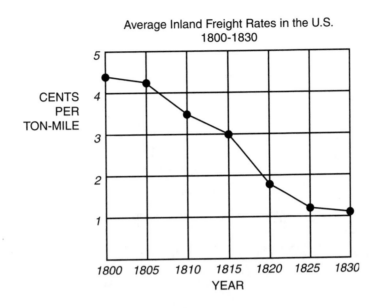

Average Inland Freight Rates in the U.S.
1800-1830

Questions

1. In 1815 how many cents per ton-mile was the freight rate?

    _____

    _____

2. Applying the information from the graph, when were freight rates more favorable for customers?

    _____

    _____

Answers

1. In 1815, the freight rate was three cents per ton-mile. To find the answer look first for the year in the question, which in this case, is 1815. The years are listed horizontally across the bottom. After finding the correct year, go up until finding a dot. That dot and the numbers on the left hand side tell you how many cents per mile the rates were for 1815. In this case, the dot is on the "three."

2. Freight rates were more favorable for customers in 1830 when they were the lowest. The word "favorable" means "better." It is better for customers to have cheaper rates. In 1830 the rates were about one cent per ton-mile, the lowest of any of the years listed.

Read the following graph and answer the questions.

Executions by State
(From 1976 through June 1989)
Total: 111

State	Executions
Texas	31
Florida	21
Louisiana	18
Georgia	14
Virginia	7
Alabama	4
North Carolina	3
Utah	3
Mississippi	3
Nevada	2
South Carolina	2
Indiana	2
Missouri	1

Source: NAACP Legal Defense and Educational Fund Inc. As published by *The New York Times,* June 1989.

Questions

1. How many people in the state of Louisiana were executed between the years 1976 and 1989?

2. Which state had the least number of executions?

3. Applying the information on the graph, would a criminal be more likely to be executed in a Southern state or in the Midwest?

4. If a person had the choice of being tried for murder in the state of Florida or South Carolina, which one should he choose?

Answers

1. Eighteen people were executed between 1976 and 1989. To find the answer find the word "Louisiana" and then look for the number to its right. That number represents the number of people executed (legally killed by the state).

2. The state of Missouri had the least number of executions. Only one person was executed.

3. A criminal would be more likely to be executed in a Southern state like Texas or Georgia than in the Midwest, like in the state of Indiana.

4. The state of South Carolina because they execute fewer criminals there than in Florida.

APPLYING INFORMATION FROM MAPS

In this section you will learn how to read a map and how to apply the information from it in order to answer questions on the GED.

This section will begin with the basics of map reading. Look at the map below and answer the following questions. The map shows colonial empires in Africa in 1914.

Questions

1. What country controlled the island off the coast of Africa?

    _____

    _____

2. Which country had less influence, Belgium or Spain?

    _____

    _____

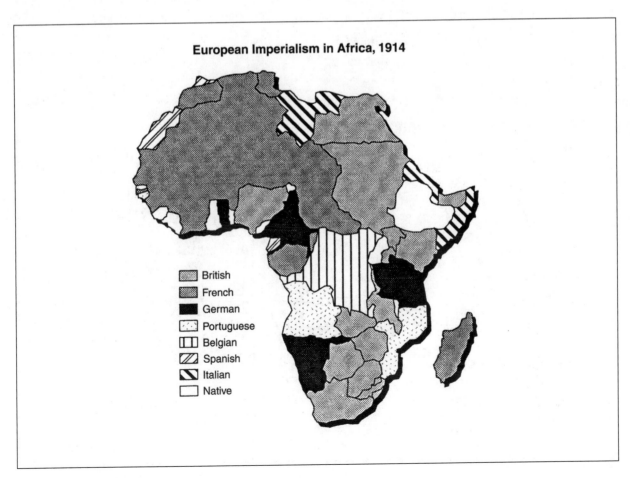

European Imperialism in Africa, 1914

British
French
German
Portuguese
Belgian
Spanish
Italian
Native

3. What country influenced the large section on the top left of the continent?

_____

_____

Answers

1. France controlled the island off the coast of Africa. To find the answer look at the key to the lower left of the map. This key tells you what the symbol for each country will be in the map.

2. Spain had less influence than Belgium. To find the answer, look at the key to find the symbol for Belgium. Then look at the map to see how much of it is covered with that symbol. Then do the same for Spain. Compare the two.

3. That area was controlled by France.

Try another example. The following map shows the number of electoral votes that each

state had in 2000. The number of electoral votes is indicative of the population of each state. The number of electoral votes is based on the number of each state's congressmen and senators combined.

Questions

1. How many votes did Texas have in 2000?

_____

_____

2. Which state received more electoral votes, Florida or California?

_____

_____

3. What are the states that are separated from the rest of the country in the lower left of the map? Why are they there?

_____

_____

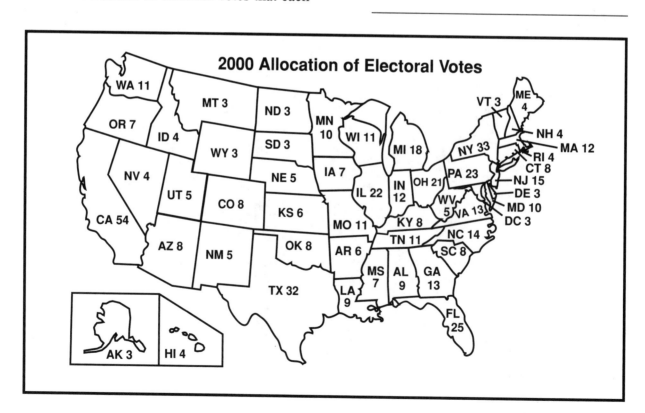

Answers

1.   Texas had 32 votes in 2000. To find the answer, find the state of Texas. If you do not know where it is, look for its abbreviation, which is "TX." If you do not know the abbreviation, look for an abbreviation that looks like it seems right.

2.   California received more electoral votes, with 54. Florida only had 25. To find the answer, locate the two states. The abbreviation for California is "CA," you can look for an abbreviation that seems correct even if you are not sure what it is. The abbreviation for Florida is "FL."

3.   They are the states of Hawaii and Alaska. These states are not actually located in the southwest of the United States, but are many miles away from the mainland. Mapmakers usually place them there for convenience sake when dealing with something specific like maps of electoral votes.

  The following map depicts the United States after the Missouri Compromise of 1820. Look at it and answer the questions that follow.

Questions

1.   Was the state of South Carolina a free state or a slave state?

_____

_____

2.   Was the state of Indiana a slave state or a free state?

_____

_____

3.   How many slave states and territories were there?

_____

_____

  We will now combine basic map reading skills with applications of those skills in order to answer a more difficult question. Use the map below again to answer the following.

4.   Knowing that Lincoln was an abolitionist (anti-slavery), which territories or states would be more likely to vote for him?

_____

_____

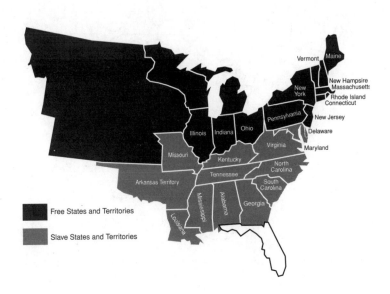

Answers

1. It was a slave state. To find the answer, look at the key in the lower left corner. That key shows you what color free and slave states will be on the map.

2. It was a free state. To find the answer, look at the key in the lower left corner. That key shows you what color free and slave states will be on the map.

3. There were twelve slave states and one territory. They include Missouri, Louisiana, Mississippi, Alabama, Tennessee, Kentucky, Georgia, South Carolina, North Carolina, Virginia, Maryland, Delaware, and the Arkansas Territory.

4. The free states, shaded in the darker color on the map, would be more likely to vote for Lincoln.

    The following is a map of Africa. Look at it and then answer the questions that follow.

Questions

1. Is the country labeled number 1 in the southern part of the continent or in the eastern?

    _____

    _____

2. What do all of the countries labeled with numbers have in common geographically?

    _____

    _____

Answers

1. It is located in the southern part of Africa.

2. They are all on the coast of the continent.

Look at the following and answer the subsequent questions.

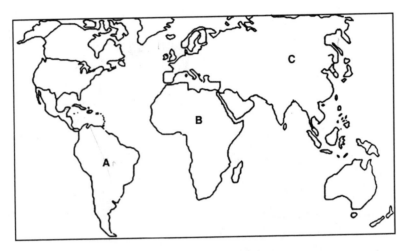

Questions

1. What does this map show?

    _____

    _____

2. What continent is labeled "B"?

    _____

    _____

Answers

1. The map shows the world.

2. The continent labeled with the letter "B" is Africa.

    Read the following map and answer the questions on the following page.

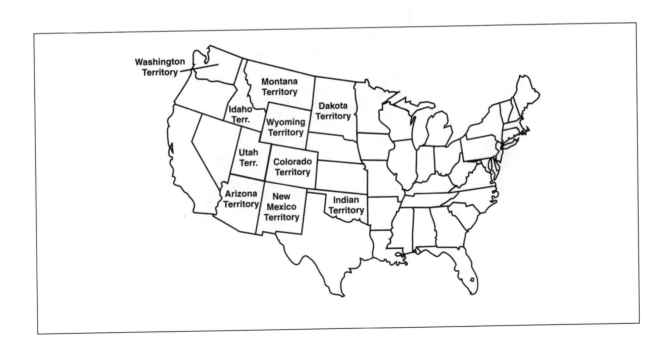

Questions

1. What territory is directly north of the New Mexico territory on the map?

_____

_____

2. Although not labeled, what future state is south of Indian territory?

_____

_____

Answers

1. The Colorado territory is located directly north of the New Mexico territory.

2. The future state of Texas is located south of Indian territory.

The map below shows Central America. Look at it carefully and then answer the questions on the following page.

Questions

1. What country is to the south of Nicaragua?

   _____

   _____

2. If the sun sets in the West, which country is the last to see the sun go down?

   _____

   _____

Answers

1. The country of Costa Rica is south of Nicaragua.

2. Mexico is the last country to see the sun go down.

APPLYING INFORMATION FROM POLITICAL CARTOONS

In this section you will be introduced to reading political cartoons and you will also learn how to apply this skill to answering questions on the Social Studies GED.

One of the basic rules in understanding a political cartoon is to watch for sarcasm. The following situation would be an example of sarcasm: A picture of a person, after an automobile accident, in the hospital with all of his limbs broken. The nurse comes in and asks how the patient is feeling and the patient says "I've never felt better." The patient does not really mean that he has never felt better, but is being sarcastic.

Another common tool to reading political cartoons, especially those based on United States history, is to understand that "Uncle Sam" represents the government. Therefore, if Uncle Sam is portrayed as going to war then the political cartoon is probably referring to the United States going to war.

Another tool is to look at the positions of the characters in the cartoons. If someone is on top of someone else, the cartoonist is probably portraying the one on top as more powerful or bullying the other. The one on the bottom might be overpowered or weak.

Start this section by looking at the following political cartoon.

This cartoon is about the Reconstruction period of United States history. The period occurred after the Civil War when slavery was no longer legal. Many Southerners were not pleased with the outcome of the war. They wanted to retain slavery.

Questions

1. What tree is the former slave holding on to?

2. What part of the country is the man in the water from and what does he think about blacks?

3. What point of view does the other man, standing to the right, have?

4. What is the cartoonist trying to say about Reconstruction?

Answers

1. The former slave is holding on to the "Tree of Liberty."

2 He is a Southerner who does not want the black man's help although he will drown if he does not accept his help.

3. He believes that the man drowning should accept the black man's help.

4. The cartoonist wants Southern whites to change their attitudes about blacks in order to reconcile with them.

The following cartoon was drawn by Benjamin Franklin in 1754. Remember that the colonies were not fully united until after the American Revolution of 1776.

JOIN, or DIE.

Questions

1. What about the abbreviations in the cartoon do you notice?

2. What could the caption be referring to?

3. What, then, does the snake represent?

Answers

1. They are abbreviations for colonies. For example, "N.Y." stands for the colony of New York.

2. The caption could be referring to colonial unity; otherwise, the union will not survive.

3.   The snake represents the thirteen colonies that Franklin wants to see united.

The following political cartoon is about politics in the United States and was drawn by the famous cartoonist Thomas Nast. Remember to look at the small print to see what the words or phrases mean.

"The Upright Bench," Which Is Above Criticism

Questions

1.   Where does the cartoon take place?

_____

_____

2.   What does the small print say in the "politics" sign?

_____

_____

3.   What is the man on top of the bench holding in his hand?

_____

_____

4.   What is the meaning of the cartoon?

_____

_____

Answers

1.   The cartoon takes place in a courthouse. Look at the words over the doorway depicted in the cartoon to get the answer.

2.   It says: *Above this line criticism stops.*

3.   The man is holding a bag full of money.

4.   The man with the money was able to buy political favors from a judge or some other court official.

APPLYING INFORMATION FROM OTHER PRACTICAL DOCUMENTS

Practical documents can be difficult to understand. Again, try to get the overall feeling of the document. Begin by simply looking for a title. Does it say "map" or "application" or any other key word? Next, look for a reference point. For example, if it is a map, look to see if it is a map of the United States, Europe, or some other region. If it is an application look to see if it is for voter registration, a job, or something else. If it is a chart or graph look for a reference point. Is it giving dates, financial figures, types of people, or some other item?

This book will help you to learn how to answer questions based on practical documents. Besides using this book, there are other ways in which you can practice the skills necessary to understand practical documents. Practical documents are all around us. You can look at different kinds of maps, street maps, country maps, world atlases. Statistical charts can be found in many sources, including governmental documents like unemployment reports. You can find tax forms, job applications, surveys, and voter registration documents on the web or in a library. Political cartoons can be found in politically oriented magazines and advertisements and in almost any magazine. Charts or graphs can be found in financial reports, reference books, and in other sources. Look at all of these documents and try to answer the following questions. What is this about? What is the main idea or opinion being expressed? You can also apply some of the types of questions used in this book to documents you find on your own.

Read the following passage and answer the questions.

Do you support the collection of sales tax on purchases made through the internet? **YES** or **NO?**

PRO: Supporters of this proposal say it is only fair to collect sales tax on purchases made, since traditional brick and mortar stores must collect such taxes. Therefore, brick and mortar stores face unfair competition from internet stores that do not collect sales tax from customers. Michigan consumers purchased an estimated $7.3 billion in 1999 through remote sales and this figure is only expected to climb. It is estimated that Michigan lost an estimated $173 million in sales tax from these remote purchases. Also, state law already states that a consumer is responsible for paying sales tax on purchases made through a catalog or out-of-state business. This "use tax" money has to be reported on an individual's state income tax form.

CON: Opponents claim that requiring sales tax on purchases made through the internet will slow the growth of the internet and cause many dot-com businesses to fail. The states, however, cannot force internet retailers to collect and pay the taxes nationwide without action by Congress since that is a matter of interstate commerce, and until that happens, the states should leave collecting internet sales tax alone.

Questions

1. What issue does this "Pro and Con" statement deal with?

_____

_____

_____

2. What does the term "use tax" refer to in the "Pro" position?

_____

_____

_____

Answers

1. The issue is whether or not sales taxes should be placed on internet purchases. The document asks, "Do you support the collection of sales tax on purchases made through the Internet?" Although other types of purchases are mentioned in the course of the argument, only internet purchases are at issue.

2. The key element here is the phrase "catalog or out-of-state business," appearing in the next to last sentence, which suggests other types of "remote" purchases in addition to those from a catalog, and therefore includes internet purchases. Furthermore, "out of state" refers to retailers other than those located in Michigan; the latter are required by the state to collect sales taxes on sales to Michigan residents, although this is not mentioned in the statement. The "use tax" is paid by the purchaser on his or her income tax form rather than being collected by the retailer.

REVIEW

In this chapter we have had a lot of practice applying information from charts, graphs, maps, and political cartoons. These are all sources of information that we must be comfortable with if we wish to move on to GED test questions. The more we practice using these sources of information the more comfortable we will become with them. Practice involves looking at the source and taking out all the important information that it gives us. It also involves understanding why the chart, graph, map, or political cartoon was made and what it is trying to tell us.

Now practice your skills of reading charts, graphs, maps, political cartoons, applications, tax forms, and other practical documents by answering the questions that follow.

☞ **Practice: Applying Information**

DIRECTIONS: Refer to the information provided and answer the questions that follow.

Questions 1–5 refer to the following chart.

Unemployment (Numbers in thousands and percentage of appropriate work force)				
	Germany		Great Britain	
1930	3,076	15.3%	1,917	14.6%
1932	5,575	30.1%	2,745	22.5%
1934	2,718	14.9%	2,159	17.7%
1936	2,151	11.6%	1,755	14.3%
1938	429	2.1%	1,191	13.3%

1. In 1934 how many people in Germany were unemployed?

    _____

    _____

2. What percent of England's work force was unemployed in 1930?

    _____

    _____

3. Applying information from the chart, in which country would a person be more likely to have a job in 1938?

    _____

    _____

4. Which country had a 22.5% unemployment rate in 1932?

    _____

    _____

5. What great change do you see in Germany that is not present in Great Britain?

    _____

    _____

Questions 6–8 refer to the following chart.

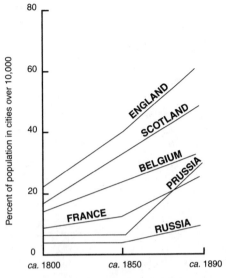

The Urbanization of Europe

6. Which country had the greater population in cities in 1890: Russia or Prussia?

_____

_____

7. In around 1800, which country had more of its population in cities than any of the other countries listed?

_____

_____

8. Applying information from the graph, which country probably had the largest percent of its population living in cities at the start of the 20th century (1900s)?

_____

_____

Questions 9–11 refer to the following map.

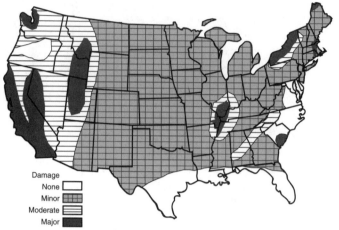

Damage
None
Minor
Moderate
Major

Seismic risk map for the U.S. issued January 1969, showing earthquake damage areas of reasonable expectancy in the next 100 years (Derived from U.S. Coast and Geodetic Survey, ESSA Rel. ES-1, January 14, 1969).

9. Do people living in Florida have to be afraid of experiencing an earthquake?

_____

_____

10. In which area of the country does the most seismic activity seem to occur?

_____

_____

11. Does the map show that the central part of the United States is free from earthquake activity?

_____

_____

Questions 12–13 refer to the following cartoon.

President McKinley (the tailor) measures Uncle Sam for a new suit to fit the fattening results of his imperial appetite.

12. What are the two phrases that are legible behind the tailor?

_____

_____

13. What does Uncle Sam's need for a larger suit represent?

_____

_____

Questions 14–17 refer to the following application.

Print clearly in Ink-Use ball-point pen or marker

Qualifications of an Eligible Applicant

You must be a citizen of the United States and, by the date of the next election, at least 18 years old and a resident of New Jersey and your county for at least 30 days.

The Commissioner of Registration will notify you upon receipt of this form.

The Registration deadline to vote at the next election is 29 days prior to election day.

Check if you wish to be a board worker/poll clerk in future elections. ❑

Check if you are permanently disabled, unable to go to the polls to vote, and wish to receive information on an Absentee Ballot. ❑

Sign or Mark ➡

If applicant is unable to complete this form, print name and address of individual who completed this form.

State of New Jersey
County Commissioners of Registration

76

Voter Registration Application

1 Check one: ❑ New Registration ❑ Address Change ❑ Name Change

2 Last Name | First Name | Middle Initial | Jr. Sr. | II III

3 Street Address Where You Live | Apt. #

4 City or Town | County | Zip Code

5 Address Where You Get Your Mail (if different from above)

6 Date of Birth- Month, Day, Year | 7 Telephone Number (optional)

8 Name And Address Of Your Last Voter Registration | County

9 Declaration - I swear or affirm that:
- I am a U.S. citizen
- I live at the above address
- I will be at least 18 years old on or before the next election
- I am not on parole, probation or serving sentence due to a conviction for an indictable offense under any federal or state laws.
- I understand that any false or fraudulent registration may subject me to a fine up to $1,000, imprisonment up to 5 years or both pursuant to R.S. 19:34-1.

For Office Use Only
Clerk
Registration No.
Office Time Stamp

Signature or Mark | Date

10 Name
Address

14. What is this application form for?

_____

_____

15. Who qualifies to fill out this form?

_____

_____

16. Does the applicant need to be able to write in order to apply?

_____

_____

17. How will the applicant know if the form was received?

_____

_____

Answers

1. 2,718,000. To find the answer find the year 1934 and look at the numbers that correspond with it in the Germany column. The number that you see is "2718." The writing above the chart says that the numbers are in thousands. This means you add three zeros to each number to get the actual number.

2. 14.6% of England's work force was unemployed. You know that the answer should

be written in percents because the subtitle of the chart (which reads *Numbers in thousands and percentage of appropriate work force*) tells you that the numbers with decimal points are percents.

3. Germany. Germany's unemployment rate was 2.1% in 1938 while Great Britain's was 13.3%. This means that fewer people were out of work in Germany, therefore, a person would be more likely to have a job in Germany than in Great Britain.

4. Great Britain.

5. The German unemployment rate drops drastically in 1938. Great Britain does not have the same fortune.

6. Prussia had more of its population in cities. Find the answer by looking at the lines that extend along with the countries' names. The lines that are higher have the greatest populations, as is explained to you along the left hand side of the graph where it says "percent of population in cities."

7. England.

8. England probably had the largest percent living in cities. In 1890 England had the most, and the start of the 20th century is only 10 years away from 1890. Ten year increments shown on the graph do not drastically change the standings of the different countries, so another ten years would most likely keep England at the top.

9. No, they have very little to fear. Florida is the state in the lower right hand corner of the country, which is only shaded a little bit. Look at the key to see what the shading means.

10. The western part of the country experiences the most seismic activity.

11. No, it only shows that there is a minor chance of an earthquake.

12. The phrases are: "national expansion" and "foreign policy."

13. He is getting heavier because of his national expansion and foreign policies. He is taking over countries during his expansion and this is also expanding his waistline. The cartoon does not explicitly (obviously) say it, but the cartoon is about the Spanish American war.

14. It is a voter registration form, as it states above column 1. In order to be eligible to vote, a person must first fill out this form.

15. In order to qualify, a person must be a U.S. citizen, live at the address on the form, be at least 18 years old before the next election, not be on parole, probation, or serving a jail sentence, and a resident of New Jersey. All of the above is written in column 9, except for the New Jersey resident requirement. That is written to the left of columns 1-3.

16. No, someone can complete the form for someone else. This is written to the left of column 10 where it says, "If applicant is unable to complete this form, print name and address of individual who completed this form."

17. The Commissioner of Registration will notify the applicant when they receive it. The answer is written to the left of column 5.

Social Studies

Post-Test

SOCIAL STUDIES

POST-TEST

DIRECTIONS: Read each of the following passages below and then answer the questions pertaining to them. Choose the <u>best answer choice</u> for each question.

Questions 1–3 are based on the following passage.

    Thomas Jefferson, a Republican, became President in 1800. Jefferson and his followers wanted American society to be very different from European society. Jefferson wanted America to be a land of independent farmers that lived under a government that did not have too much control over their lives. America would be free of the industrial and urban (city-like) problems of European cities because America would remain rural (farm-like).

1. In what year was Thomas Jefferson elected President?

    (1)   1804.

    (2)   1700.

    (3)   1808.

    (4)   1800.

    (5)   1900.

2. What kind of government did Jefferson hope for?

    (1)   One that did not have too much control over people's lives.

    (2)   One that had a lot of control over people's lives.

    (3)   A democratic one.

    (4)   An urban one.

    (5)   A European one.

3. When Jefferson compared Europe to America, what did he see?

    (1)   America would have more cities.

    (2)   America as a rural area and Europe as an urban area.

    (3)   Europe was near the ocean but America was not.

    (4)   Europe was not Republican, America was.

    (5)   America was industrial and Europe was not.

Questions 4 and 5 are based on the following passage.

    The Truman Doctrine was written to contain, or hold still, communist expansion because the American government was opposed to communism. The Truman Doctrine allowed countries that were not communist to receive

American aid so that they would not fall to that form of government. The Doctrine originally came about in response to Greek and Turkish requests for aid in fighting off communists.

4. Which of the following best describes the purpose of the Truman Doctrine?

    (1) To contain communist expansion.

    (2) To create more communist countries.

    (3) To help the Greeks win a war with the Turks.

    (4) To give aid to all countries in need.

    (5) To expand communism.

5. What was the American government opposed to?

    (1) Greeks.

    (2) Turks.

    (3) Doctrines.

    (4) Aid.

    (5) Communism.

Questions 6–8 are based on the following table.

Comparison of Population in Selected Cities in the United States—1988

City	Population
New York	7,352,700
Los Angeles	3,352,710
Chicago	2,977,520
Houston	1,698,090
Philadelphia	1,647,000
San Diego	1,070,310

6. What was the population of New York in 1988?

    (1) 3,352,710.

    (2) 1,070,310.

    (3) 2,000,000.

    (4) It does not say.

    (5) 7,352,700.

7. Which city had the smallest population?

    (1) New York.

    (2) Chicago.

    (3) San Diego.

    (4) Houston.

    (5) Philadelphia.

8. Approximately how much larger was the population of New York than the population of Los Angeles in 1988?

    (1) 3,500,000

    (2) 3,000,000

    (3) 4,000,000

    (4) 2,800,000

    (5) 5,000,000

Questions 9–11 are based on the following passage.

There are two groups in America that are growing at a very fast pace. One group is the single-parent families group. This group represents over 26% of the families nationwide. Most of the single-parent families are headed by women. Another group that is growing quickly is the over-65-year-old group. This is the fastest growing group in the country. Some of the problems of this age group are poor medical care and loneliness.

9. What two groups are growing at a fast pace?

    (1) Poor medical care and loneliness.

(2)   Single-parent families and women.

(3)   Women and 65 year olds.

(4)   Children and single-parent families.

(5)   Single-parent families and people age 65 and over.

10.   What are some problems of the 65 and over group?

(1)   Poor medical care and loneliness.

(2)   Growing quickly.

(3)   Having single-parent families.

(4)   Poor medical care and aging.

(5)   Loneliness and living in America.

11.   Which number best describes how many of America's families are single-parent families?

(1)   One half.

(2)   Almost one third.

(3)   90%.

(4)   None.

(5)   46%.

Questions 12–14 are based on the following passage.

Texas is the second-largest state in the United States. Texas covers 261,797 square miles and 254 counties. Texas has many different types of terrains such as piney woods, post oak belt, plains, rolling prairie, high plains, valley, coastal prairie, and West Texas. The population of Texas in 2000 was over 20 million. Texas is one of the most beautiful states in the country.

12.   How many square miles does Texas cover?

(1)   271,697.

(2)   261,797.

(3)   250,000.

(4)   254.

(5)   245.

13.   Which of the following types of terrain does Texas *not* have?

(1)   High plains.

(2)   Valley.

(3)   Desert.

(4)   Coastal prairie.

(5)   Piney woods.

14.   In 2000, the number of people living in Texas was

(1)   nearly 20 million.

(2)   261,797.

(3)   exactly 20 million.

(4)   greater than 20 million.

(5)   over 4 million.

Questions 15–18 refer to the following map.

Free States and Territories

Slave States and Territories

Areas at first free, later open to slavery

15. Which of the following was a slave state?

   (1) California.

   (2) Texas.

   (3) The Oregon territory.

   (4) Michigan.

   (5) Wisconsin.

16. Which of the following was a free state?

   (1) Iowa.

   (2) Alabama.

   (3) Florida.

   (4) Missouri.

   (5) Louisiana.

17. What are the two areas that were at first free, and then open to slavery?

   (1) Texas and the Kansas territory.

   (2) The Utah territory and Iowa.

   (3) The Nebraska and Kansas territory.

   (4) Illinois and Indiana.

   (5) Georgia and Ohio.

18. In which state would a black person be free?

   (1) Tennessee.

   (2) Texas.

   (3) New York.

   (4) Florida.

   (5) Missouri.

Questions 19–21 refer to the following passage.

Many different ethnic groups settled in colonial America. The Germans, known as the Pennsylvania Dutch, settled in Pennsylvania. The French settled in New York. The Scots-Irish settled in the Middle and Southern colonies. The Dutch and English settled in New York. Spanish and Portuguese Jews settled in the urban areas of New York, Rhode Island, and South Carolina.

19. Which group settled in the Middle and Southern colonies?

    (1) The French.

    (2) The Scots-Irish.

    (3) Spanish and Portuguese Jews.

    (4) The Dutch.

    (5) The English.

20. By inferring meanings, in which state would the most people speak German?

    (1) South Carolina.

    (2) New York.

    (3) Pennsylvania.

    (4) Rhode Island.

    (5) The Middle colonies.

21. Which group migrated towards urban areas?

    (1) The Dutch.

    (2) Germans.

    (3) The French.

    (4) Spanish and Portuguese Jews.

    (5) Scots-Irish.

Questions 22–24 refer to the following passage.

The Persian Gulf War was fought between January and April of 1991. It was fought because Saddam Hussein of Iraq invaded the country of Kuwait. The United States, with the aid of many other nations, forced the Iraqis out of Kuwait.

22. Who invaded the country of Kuwait?

    (1) The United States.

    (2) The U.S.

    (3) Saddam Hussein.

    (4) Iran.

    (5) The Persians.

23. In this case, what does the word "aid" mean?

    (1) Weapons.

    (2) Help.

    (3) Airplanes.

    (4) Computers.

    (5) Advice.

24. By May of 1992, the Persian Gulf War was

    (1) at its height.

    (2) slowing down.

    (3) about to begin.

    (4) still going on.

    (5) over.

Questions 25–27 refer to the following passages.

The following is an excerpt from a famous Supreme Court case called *Brown v. Board of Education of Topeka*. It ended segregation of black and white Americans in public education. This excerpt is taken from the historical opinion of Chief Justice Warren.

"Segregation of white and colored children in public schools has a detrimental effect upon the colored children. The impact is greater when it has the sanction of the law, for the policy of separating the races is usually interpreted as denoting the inferiority of the negro group. A sense of inferiority affects the motivation of a child to learn. Segregation with the sanction of law, therefore, has a tendency to [retard] the educational and mental development of negro children and to deprive them of some of the benefits they would receive in a racial[ly] integrated school system."

25. The word "retard" in this context means

    (1) speed up.

    (2) slow down.

    (3) get rid of.

    (4) investigate.

    (5) travel.

26. Chief Justice Warren is concluding that black children

    (1) should never go to college.

    (2) are inferior to white children.

    (3) are being harmed by segregated schools.

    (4) should become lawyers.

    (5) are helped by being in segregated schools.

27. Chief Justice Warren is concerned that when a child feels inferior he or she

    (1) will want to go to a segregated school.

    (2) will disobey the law.

    (3) will have children with learning difficulties.

    (4) does not feel motivated to learn.

    (5) does not want to be with his or her own race.

Questions 28–30 refer to the following passage.

The Civil War, which started in 1861 and ended in 1865, was the bloodiest war in U.S. history. The war was fought over political and social differences between the Union and the Confederacy. The war ended the institution of slavery in America.

Some of the states in the Confederacy were South Carolina, Georgia, and Florida. Some of the states in the Union were Pennsylvania, Ohio, and New York.

28. The Civil War began in

    (1) 1859.

    (2) 1860.

    (3) 1861.

    (4) 1862.

    (5) 1863.

29. Which of the following was a state in the Union?

    (1) Ohio.

    (2) Texas.

    (3) Georgia.

    (4) Florida.

    (5) Oregon.

30. What caused the end of slavery in America?

    (1) The Confederacy.

    (2) U.S. history.

    (3) Institutions.

    (4) The Civil War.

    (5) The Union.

Questions 31 and 32 refer to the following form.

a Control number	22222	Void ☐	For Official Use Only ☐ OMB No. 1545-0008		
b Employer identification number			1 Wages, tips, other compensation $	2 Federal income tax withheld $	
c Employer's name, address, and ZIP code			3 Social security wages $	4 Social security tax withheld $	
			5 Medicare wages and tips $	6 Medicare tax withheld $	
			7 Social security tips $	8 Allocated tips $	
d Employee's social security number			9 Advance EIC payment $	10 Dependent care benefits $	
e Employee's first name and initial	Last name		11 Nonqualified plans $	12a See instructions for box 12 $	
			13 Statutory employee ☐ Retirement plan ☐ Third-party sick pay ☐	12b $	
			14 Other	12c $	
				12d $	
f Employee's address and ZIP code					
15 State Employer's state ID number	16 State wages, tips, etc. $	17 State income tax $	18 Local wages, tips, etc. $	19 Local income tax $	20 Locality name
	$	$	$	$	

Form **W-2** **Wage and Tax Statement**   **2001**   Department of the Treasury—Internal Revenue Service

For Privacy Act and Paperwork Reduction Act Notice, see separate instructions.

Copy A For Social Security Administration—Send this entire page with Form W-3 to the Social Security Administration; photocopies are **not** acceptable.

Cat. No. 10134D

Do Not Cut, Fold, or Staple Forms on This Page — Do Not Cut, Fold, or Staple Forms on This Page

31. In which box is the employee's state income tax withholding listed?

    (1) Box #2.

    (2) Box #3.

    (3) Box #16.

    (4) Box #17.

    (5) Box #19.

32. The W-2 Form states that the information on the form is being furnished to the Internal Revenue Service which is part of what branch of the Federal Government?

    (1) Department of State.

    (2) Department of Interior.

    (3) Department of the Treasury.

    (4) Department of Justice.

    (5) Department of Commerce.

SOCIAL STUDIES

ANSWER KEY

1. (4)	9. (5)	17. (3)	25. (2)
2. (1)	10. (1)	18. (3)	26. (3)
3. (2)	11. (2)	19. (2)	27. (4)
4. (1)	12. (2)	20. (3)	28. (3)
5. (5)	13. (3)	21. (4)	29. (1)
6. (5)	14. (4)	22. (3)	30. (4)
7. (3)	15. (2)	23. (2)	31. (4)
8. (3)	16. (1)	24. (5)	32. (3)

POST-TEST SELF-EVALUATION

Question Number	Subject Matter Tested	Section to Study (section, heading)
1.	reading comprehension	II
2.	reading comprehension	II
3.	reading comprehension	II
4.	important details	II, Asking Who, What, Where, and When
5.	reading comprehension	II
6.	facts and opinions	IV, Distinguishing Fact from Opinion
7.	reading graphs	V, Applying Information from Graphs
8.	reading graphs	V, Applying Information from Graphs
9.	reading comprehension	II
10.	reading comprehension	II
11.	reading comprehension	II
12.	reading comprehension	II
13.	reading comprehension	II
14.	fact or opinion	IV, Distinguishing Fact from Opinion
15.	reading comprehension	II
16.	reading comprehension	II, Using Context Clues to Figure Out Unfamiliar Words
17.	reading comprehension	II, Using Context Clues to Figure Out Unfamiliar Words
18.	recognizing sequences	IV, Identifying Sequences
19.	identify cause and effect relationships	IV, Cause and Effect Relationships
20.	identify cause and effect relationships	IV, Cause and Effect Relationships
21.	reading comprehension	II
22.	inference	IV, Inferring Meaning
23.	political cartoons	II, Using Context Clues to Figure Out Unfamiliar Words V, Applying Information from Political Cartoons
24.	political cartoons	V, Applying Information from Political Cartoons

II = Comprehending What You Read   III = Graphs and Charts   IV = Reading Patterns   V = Applying Information

Question Number	Subject Matter Tested	Section to Study (section, heading)
25.	reading comprehension	II, Using Context Clues to Figure Out Unfamiliar Words
26.	reading comprehension	II
27.	reading comprehension	II
28.	reading comprehension	II, Asking Who, What, Where, and When
29.	reading comprehension	II, Asking Who, What, Where, and When
30.	reading comprehension	II
31.	reading a table	III, Interpreting Data
32.	reading a table	III, Interpreting Data

II = Comprehending What You Read   III = Graphs and Charts   IV = Reading Patterns   V = Applying Information

POST-TEST
ANSWERS AND EXPLANATIONS

1. **(4)** The answer is in the first sentence of the passage, which reads, *Thomas Jefferson, a Republican, became President in 1800.* The year 1800 is the only year mentioned in the passage.

2. **(1)** The answer can be found in the sentence that reads, *Jefferson wanted America to be a land of independent farmers that lived under a government that did not have too much control over their lives.* Choice (2) is incorrect because the above sentence directly contradicts it. (3) is incorrect because the word "democracy" is not mentioned. (4) is incorrect because Jefferson wanted a rural world, not an urban one. (5) is incorrect because Jefferson wanted America to not be like Europe.

3. **(2)** Jefferson wanted America to be a rural area, different from European urban cities. This can be found in the last sentence of the passage.

4. **(1)** The choice can be found in the first sentence, which reads, *The Truman Doctrine was written to contain, or hold still, communist expansion because the American government was opposed to communism.*

5. **(5)** The American government was opposed to communism, as the first sentence tells you.

6. **(5)** The population of New York was 7,352,700.

7. **(3)** San Diego had the smallest population.

8. **(3)** The approximate difference between the two populations is 4 million. You can round the numbers off to get 7 million and 3 million and find the difference, or you may have noticed that 352,700 and 352,710 are so close that the exact difference is very near 4 million. (The actual difference is 3,999,990.)

9. **(5)** The choice can be found in two different sentences. One reads, *One group is the single-parent families group.* The other reads, *Another group that is growing quickly is the over-65-year-old group.*

10. **(1)** The choice can be found in the sentence that reads, *Some of the problems of this age group are poor medical care and loneliness.*

11. **(2)** The passage tells you that 26% of families are single-parent families. 26% is almost one-third.

12. **(2)** The correct choice can be found in the sentence that reads, *Texas covers 261,797 square miles and 254 counties.*

13. **(3)** The correct choice can be found by reading the list of types of physical regions that Texas does have and comparing that list to the possible choices.

14. **(4)** The only choice that can be correct is (4). As stated in the passage, the population is over 20 million.

15. **(2)** The state of Texas is shaded in black, which, according to the map key, indicates a slave state. None of the other possible choices are shaded in black.

16. **(1)** The state of Iowa is shaded in light gray, which indicates a free state. None of the other possible choices are shaded in light gray.

17. **(3)** The Nebraska and Kansas territories are shaded in medium gray, which, according to the map key, indicates areas that were at first free and later opened to slavery.

18. **(3)** A black person would have been free in New York. The other states are all shaded in black, so they are slave states.

19. **(2)** The choice can be found in the sentence that reads, *The Scots-Irish settled in the Middle and Southern colonies.*

20. **(3)** The correct choice can be found in the sentence that reads, *The Germans, known as the Pennsylvania Dutch, settled in Pennsylvania.*

21. **(4)** The correct choice can be found in the sentence that reads, *Spanish and Portuguese Jews settled in the urban areas of New York, Rhode Island, and South Carolina.*

22. **(3)** Saddam Hussein of Iraq invaded Kuwait.

23. **(2)** In this case, the word "aid" means "help."

24. **(5)** The war was fought between January and April of 1992, which implies that by May of 1992 it was over.

25. **(2)** "Retard" in this context means to "slow down."

26. **(3)** The answer can be found in many key phrases including *detrimental effect* and *a sense of inferiority affects the motivation of a child to learn.*

27. **(4)** The answer can be found in the third sentence of the passage.

28. **(3)** The correct choice is in the first sentence, which reads, *The Civil War, which started in 1861 and ended in 1865, was the bloodiest war in U.S. history.*

29. **(1)** Ohio was a state in the Union, as the last sentence of the passage tells you.

30. **(4)** The correct choice can be found in the sentence that reads, *The war ended the institution of slavery in America.*

31. **(4)** Although it does not use the term "withholding," box #17 lists the amount withheld for state income tax. Box #2 is for Federal income tax withholding. Box #3 is for wages subject to Social Security. Box #16 is for wages subject to state income tax, and box #19 is for local income tax withholding.

32. **(3)** At the bottom of the form on the lower right hand corner are the words "Department of Treasury–Internal Revenue Service."

Appendix: Glossary of Terms

SOCIAL STUDIES

APPENDIX: GLOSSARY OF TERMS

General Terms

adopted—to take as one's own.

Allies—during World War I and II, the side that included Great Britain, France, Russia (which was the Soviet Union by World War II), and the United States.

American Revolution—the revolt of the American colonists against their ruler, King George III of England.

appalled—dismayed, concerned.

authorized—to give official approval or power.

Black Death—another name for bubonic plague.

Brown vs. Board of Education—a case decided by the Supreme Court in 1954 which ruled that the school board in Topeka, Kansas, could not segregate pupils.

bubonic plague—a contagious, usually fatal disease, transmitted by fleas.

campaign—a series of military operations.

Cheyenne—a nomadic tribe of Plains Indians.

collective behavior—group behavior outside of normal behavior.

Commander-in-Chief—the supreme commander of all the armed forces of a nation; in the U.S., it is the President.

communist—a person who believes that all property, business, and goods are owned by the state.

Confederacy—the alliance of Southern states during the American Civil War (1861–1865).

confidence—trust.

confronted—faced with, presented.

context—the sentence or paragraph in which a word or group of words occurs.

Continental Army—the American colonists who revolted against England's King George III in the American Revolution.

controversial—something or someone whose ideas, worth, practices can be disputed or debated.

corrupt—immoral, perverted, ruin.

culture—behavioral characteristics among a group of people.

D-Day—June 6, 1944, the day of the Allied invasion of Normandy, France.

debate—deliberation, discussion of opposing views.

decipher—to interpret, to determine.

disallow—to not allow or to refuse to allow.

discretionary income—household money not earmarked for regular expenses such as rent, utilities, etc.

dominated—controlled, outnumbered.

educational attainment—the highest grade level a person has achieved.

electoral college—group of electors representing their states who choose the President and Vice President. The number of electors from the state equals the number of Senators and Representatives the state sends to the U.S. Congress.

encompassed—included, contained.

engaged—became involved in.

essential—basic, necessary.

excrement—bodily waste, fecal matter.

executive branch—the branch of government that carries out laws.

fervent—very devoted or passionate.

function—how a group operates or carries out its activities.

Great Depression—a period of greatly reduced business activity in the 1930s that resulted in widespread unemployment, falling wages, and falling prices.

Gross National Product (GNP)—the total value of goods and services produced in a year by a nation.

Hiroshima—the Japanese city where the first atomic bomb was dropped by the United States during World War II, August 6, 1945.

House of Representatives—one of two sections of the United States Congress. The number of Representatives each state has is based upon its population.

inception—the start or beginning of something.

increments—increases in number or size.

inherent—existing as an essential part.

institution—an established custom or practice.

interference—to come between or to meddle.

invaded—entered by force, took over.

judicial—of, or about, judges.

judicial branch—the branch of government that decides what laws mean.

justified—warranted, correct, right.

Korean War—the 1950–1953 war between North Korea, a communist country backed by the Soviet Union, and South Korea, a capitalist country backed by the United States.

legislative branch—the branch of government that makes laws.

liberate—to free from.

majority—the greater number or part of something.

mandate—to order or command.

manifesto—a public declaration of principles or intentions.

mass hysteria—uncontrollable fear or anxiety among a group of people.

Nagasaki—the Japanese city that was the site of the second atomic bomb dropped by the United States during World War II, August 9, 1945.

nomadic—having no fixed abode or home.

nominate—to name someone to a position.

Normandy invasion—when Allied troops landed on the beaches of Normandy, France on June 6, 1944, beginning the final Allied campaign in Europe during World War II.

offended—created anger.

Okinawa—the largest of Japan's Ryukyu Islands. It was the site of a famous battle during World War II.

Operation Overlord—the code name for the Normandy invasion, which occurred on June 6, 1944.

origins—the beginnings of, how something came to be.

osmosis—learning or absorbing by utilizing the surroundings.

overturn—to turn over or to conquer.

panic—a sudden overpowering terror.

Pawnee—a sedentary tribe of Plains Indians.

Pearl Harbor—located on Oahu Island, Hawaii, it was the scene of a surprise attack on American ships, planes, and servicemen by the Japanese. This led to the United States' entrance into World War II.

Plains Indians—Native Americans who lived between the Mississippi River and the Rocky Mountains and from Southern Canada to Texas.

pledged—promised.

Plessy vs. Ferguson—a case decided by the Supreme Court in 1896 that said the state of Louisiana had the right to segregate blacks and whites in railway carriages.

previewing—looking over an article to see what it is about.

progressive—tax system that takes a greater percentage from those who have higher incomes.

projections—anticipated numbers or results.

proletariat—a member of the industrial working class.

proportional—tax system that takes the same percentage of every person's income, whether they are rich or poor.

regressive—tax system in which everyone pays the same, such as a sales tax.

Republican party—one of the two major political parties in the United States.

resurgence—rising, or being utilized again.

scientific perspective—acquiring knowledge from experience and observation.

sedentary—sitting or staying in one place.

segregate—to separate or isolate.

Senate—one of two sections of the United States Congress. Each state has two senators.

sentiment—feeling.

sophisticated—complicated.

spontaneously—happening all of a sudden, without premeditation or cause.

status quo—the existing state of affairs.

structure—organization, arrangement.

subsequent—following, coming after.

supporting sentences—sentences that help you understand the topic sentence.

Supreme Court—the highest ranking court in the United States.

surrender—to give up or abandon.

taxation—a system allowing government to take money from its citizens to fund the government.

territory—an area or region.

topic sentence—the sentence containing the main idea of a passage.

treaties—formal agreements.

Union—the alliance of Northern states during the American Civil War, 1861–1865.

urban sanitation—method of disposing of sewage and garbage in cities and towns.

urbanization—changing from rural life to city life.

veto—to reject.

World War II—the 1939–1945 war between the Allied Powers (which included Great Britain, France, the United States, and the Soviet Union) and the Axis Powers (which included Germany, Italy, and Japan).

World History Terms

World History: The Ancient World

Abraham—Founder of the Hebrews who migrated from Ur during the late second millennium.

Akkadians—A Near Eastern people who conquered the Sumerians about 2300 to 2200 B.C.; this development resulted in the cultural assimilation of the Sumerians and the Akkadians.

Akhenaton—Also known as Amenhotep IV, this Egyptian pharaoh (ca. 1360 B.C.) advanced monotheism when he argued that there was one god, Aton.

Archaic Period—A phase of Egyptian history that started with the earliest indications of Egyptian society at about 5000 B.C. and concluded when Menes (or Narmer) unified Upper and Lower Egypt about 3200 B.C. This term is also applied to a period of Greek life from 800 to 500 B.C. during which the polis (city-state) emerged and dominated Greek life.

Edict of Milan—A decree by the Roman Emperor Constantine that proclaimed Christianity as the Empire's official religion.

First Intermediate Period—A phase of Egyptian history that occurred when the Old Kingdom collapsed as a result of reaction against centralized authority (2180 B.C.); the Egyptian nobility reasserted its authority.

Gilgamesh—An epic Sumerian poem that provides historians with a valuable primary source on Sumerian culture and values.

Hellenic Age—The culture of the Greek city-states to the ascendency of Alexander the Great.

Hellenistic Age—A culture that resulted from the dissemination of Greek values and attitudes throughout the Eastern Mediterranean; it resulted from the establishment of Alexander's Empire.

Middle Kingdom—A phase of Egyptian history (2040–1785 B.C.) that is considered as a cultural watershed in ancient history.

Nebuchadnezzar—Babylonian leader who ordered the destruction of Solomon's Temple in 587 B.C. and enslaved the Jews in Babylon.

New Kingdom—A phase of Egyptian history (1560–1085 B.C.) that was characterized by Egyptian aggression into Palestine and Syria and into Nubia in the south.

Old Kingdom—A phase of Egyptian history (2685–2180 B.C.) during which pharaohs were considered gods and the Egyptian capital was moved to Memphis.

Pax Romana—The "Roman Peace" that was imposed by Roman authority between the establishment of the Empire by Octavian in 27 B.C. and the death of Marcus Aureilius in A.D. 180.

Peloponnesian War—The Greek Civil War (431–404 B.C.) with Athens and Sparta as the principal protagonists.

Persian War—Consisted of a series of conflicts between the Persians and Greek city-states (490s–480 B.C.).

Polis—Greek city-state; a structure and form of society that dominated Greek life.

Punic Wars—A series of three wars between Carthage and Rome that resulted in the establishment of Roman dominance of the central Mediterranean by 146 B.C.

Second Intermediate Period—A phase of Egyptian history during which the Middle Kingdom was destroyed by the invasion of the Hyskos (1785–1560 B.C.).

Zoroastrianism—A Persian religion that conceived of the universe as a dualism, a struggle between the gods of good and evil.

World History: The Middle Ages

Carolingian—The dynasty established by Charles the Great, or Charlemagne, at the beginning of the ninth century.

Carolingian Renaissance—A revival of learning and scholarship centered at Aix-la-Chapelle (Aachen), which was sponsored by Carolingian monarchs.

Cluniac Movement—A ninth-century church reform movement centered at Cluny, France; it stressed the need for the church to be independent of temporal rulers.

Corpus Juris Civilis—Also known as the Code of Justinian, this assembly of law was developed under the direction of the

Byzantine Emperor Justinian I during the sixth century.

Feudalism—The decentralized political system of personal ties and obligation that bound vassals to their lords.

Great Schism—A disruption within Christianity that had its origins in a dispute over differing interpretations of the Nicene Creed; in 1054 the Orthodox patriarch and the pope formalized the split between the Roman and Eastern churches by excommunicating one another.

Koran—The holy book of Islam that consists of the teachings of Mohammed.

Magna Carta—An English medieval document (1215) that forced King John to recognize the ancient rights of the nobility; it established the principle of a limited English monarch.

Manorialism—The economic system in which nobles who were granted large estates by the kings strove for self-sufficiency.

Merovingian—The Frankish dynasty established by Clovis in A.D. 481.

Reconquista—The process (1085–1492) of reducing Muslim control of Spain by the efforts of the Spanish Christian nobility.

Scholasticism—An effort to reconcile reason and faith and to instruct Christians on how to make sense of the pagan tradition.

serfs—Peasants (also called *villeins*) who were bound to the lord's land.

vassals—Members of the feudal nobility who held property and authority in accord with the king.

World History: The Renaissance

Anticlericalism—The misdeeds of the clergy and the problems of the temporal church were popular themes in Renaissance literature.

Classicism—A cultural designation characterized by symmetry, harmony, and an aesthetic element identified with Greco-Roman tradition.

Humanism—The reading and understanding of writings and ideals of the classical past.

Individualism—Renaissance individualism emphasized the "hero in history" and magnified the significance of individual acts or accomplishments.

Italian Renaissance—The Renaissance in Italy that was characterized by a genuine interest in the ancients and the pursuit of art.

Nationalism—Renaissance national identity contributed to the movement to establish nation-states in western Europe and assisted political leaders in their struggles with the church.

Northern Renaissance—The Renaissance outside of Italy that was characterized by a halfhearted interest in the ancients and by the pursuit of literary scholarship.

Renaissance—French for "rebirth"; the word describes the reawakening of interest in the heritage of the classical past.

World History: The Reformation

Anglicanism—The English Protestant movement that was embodied by Elizabethan statutes.

Catholic Reformation—The Roman Catholic response to Protestantism; the Council of Trent and the establishment of new religious orders were major elements of this movement. This was also known as the Counter-Reformation.

Consubstantiation—Lutheran concept of the Eucharist in which the body and blood of Jesus are mystically present at the Communion service.

Indulgences—The Roman Catholic doctrine that remits the temporal punishment (purgatory) due to sin.

Mysticism—An approach to spirituality that emphasizes direct communication with God and minimizes the need of the institutional church.

Predestination—Emphasized by John Calvin, it argues that God knew who would obtain salvation before those people were born.

Presbyterianism—Manifestation of Calvinism in Scotland under the leadership of John Knox.

Puritanism—English Protestant movement that was Calvinist influenced and determined to eliminate the vestiges of Romanism that existed in the Elizabethan Anglican church.

Transubstantiation—The Catholic view of the Eucharist in which the actual body and blood of Jesus is present at the Communion of the Mass.

Tridentine—Relating to the decrees and ordinances of the Council of Trent, the major component of the Catholic Reformation.

World History: Exploration, Commercialism, and the New States

Absolutism—Emphasized the role of the state and its fulfillment of some specific purpose, such as nationalism, religion, or the glory of the monarch.

Capitalism—The economic philosophy characterized by private property, profit, competition, and the institution of bank credit.

Cavaliers—Royalist supporters of the monarchy during the English Civil War.

Commercialism—The revival of trade and economic activity that emerged after the collapse of feudalism and was caused by the impact of discovery and the emergence of new nation-states.

Constitutionalism—Rules, often unwritten, defining and limiting government; it sought to enhance the liberty of the individual.

Divine Right Theory—Advocated by James I of England, it maintained the medieval notion that monarchs held office and authority by the will of God.

Huguenots—French Protestants who resisted the absolutism of the French monarchs.

Mercantilism—An economic philosophy based on a fixed amount of wealth and the maintenance of a favorable balance of trade.

Roundheads—Supporters of Parliament during the English Civil War.

Sovereignty—Concept developed by Jean Bodin; Bodin argued that in each country one power or institution must be strong enough to make everyone else obey.

Urbanization—Both a cause and result of economic growth, it required and created a network of market relationships.

World History: The New Thought

Baroque—An artistic style that was prevalent in Mediterranean cultures during the late sixteenth and early seventeenth centuries, which was characterized by a revolt against "classicism"; it lacked harmony and advanced grandeur and the spectacle in art.

deductive reasoning—Based on the principle, "general to particular."

Deism—An eighteenth-century concept that emphasized direct belief in God and denounced institutional religions.

Empiricism—The method that was based on experimentation; advocated by Francis Bacon.

Enlightened Despotism—An approach to government that maintained that the best government would be that led by an absolute monarch who was "enlightened," that is, a devotee of the rationalist principles associated with the Enlightenment.

Geocentrism—The Ptolemaic theory that the earth was the center of the universe and that the sun revolved about it.

Heliocentrism—The Copernican theory that the sun was the center of the universe and that the earth revolved about it.

Humanitarianism—A rationalist concept that argued the need for organized human intervention to resolve problems that adversely affected individuals or groups of individuals.

inductive reasoning—Related to the scientific method (empiricism), it was based on the principle "from particular to general."

Josephism—The "enlightened" approach to government undertaken during the reign of Joseph II of Austria.

Laudism—Romanist values advanced by Archbishop William Laud during the reign of Charles I of England.

Mannerism—The thematic approach of painters and sculptors in the late sixteenth century, it emphasized dramatic and emotional qualities.

Old Pretender—Designation given to James, son of James II of England; in 1715 he led an unsuccessful revolt in an attempt to restore the Catholic Stuarts.

Philosophes—A group of eighteenth-century social activists for whom knowledge was something to be converted into reform.

Progress—The cult of progress as a historical force or inevitable consequence of rationalist human organization emerged during the Enlightenment.

Rationalism—Stressed deductive reasoning or mathematical logic as the basis for their epistemology (source of knowledge).

Salon—Homes of French nobles in Paris that served as the centers for discussion of new ideas during the Enlightenment.

Secularism—A denunciation of the values and ideas associated with organized religions, it advanced a rationalist order and agenda.

Time of Troubles—An era in Russian history from the death of Ivan IV in 1584 to the emergence of the Romanov dynasty in 1613; it was a period of turmoil, famine, palace struggles, and war with Poland.

Young Pretender—Designation given to Charles Edward (Bonnie Prince Charlie), son of the "Old Pretender"; he attempted to come to power through an unsuccessful 1745 plot.

World History: Louis XIV to Frederick the Great

Balance of Power—A condition of political equilibrium among states that is sustained by limiting the power of the greatest state so that the freedom and independence of all states can be maintained.

Commonwealth—The Parliamentary-based government of England between 1649 and 1653.

Estates–General—The ancient French assembly that was based on three separate "Estates" or orders: the nobility, the church, and the people.

Grand Remonstrance—An English Parliamentary document (1641) that advanced more than 200 grievances against Charles I and demanded that his appointees be approved by Parliament.

Instrument of Government—The English document of 1653, which established the Protectorate; it was the only written constitution in English history.

Intendants—Agents of the French monarch in administering the kingdom; members of the French bureaucracy.

World History: The French Revolution

Ancien Regime—The "Old Regime" which was in power prior to the French Revolution of 1789; the term applies to conservative or reactionary regimes in other countries.

Bourgeoisie—The industrial middle class, which was divided into the upper *bourgeoisie* (bankers, merchants, and industrialists) and the lower *bourgeoisie* (small industrialists, merchants, and professionals).

Congress System—Based on the principle of collective security and the need to maintain the values of order, European states attempted to coordinate their policies to attain their common purposes (1815–1822).

Conservatism—A political belief in order, society, the state, faith, and tradition.

Consulate—The French government between 1799 and 1804, which was dominated by Napoleon who served as "First Consul."

Convention—The form of government during the most radical period of the French Revolution, 1792–1795; the most significant achievement of the Convention was to turn the tide against the invading armies of the Coalition.

Coup d'Etat Brumaire—Napoleon's overthrow of the Directory on November 9, 1799.

Declaration of the Rights of Man and the Citizen—A statement of revolutionary ideas and values developed in August 1789; a preamble of subsequent constitutions.

Directory—The French government between 1795 and 1799; it was middle class in tone and value and was a reaction against the excesses of the Convention.

Legitimacy—Belief at the Congress of Vienna that called for the restoration of "legitimate" regimes, that is, regimes that were in power prior to 1789.

Liberalism—The individual is a self-sufficient being whose freedom and well-being are the sole reasons for the existence of society.

National Assembly—The French government between the summer of 1789 and the opening session of the Legislative Assembly in 1791.

Nationalism—Based on an enhancing of the level of consciousness of people having a common language, soil, traditions, history, culture, and experience, and resulting in attempts to seek political unity around an identity of what or who constitutes the nation.

Parliaments—French courts that were controlled by the nobility; prior to the French Revolution, they were used to manipulate taxes.

World History: The Age of Realism and Materialism

Anarchism—Reacting to the consequences of the Industrial Revolution, anarchism advocated a society of no property or authority.

Eastern Question—Issues and problems relating to the collapse of the Ottoman Empire, the ambitions of Russia and Austria-Hungary in the Balkans, and the emergent nationalist aspirations of Balkan peoples.

Grossdeutsch—The "Big Germany" which included both Prussia and Austria.

Kleindeutsch—The "Small Germany" which excluded Austria.

Kulturkampf—Bismarck's campaign against the influence of the Catholic Church in the Centre Party.

Realpolitik—The "politics of the possible" was the realistic approach to diplomacy adopted by Bismarck in Prussia and Cavour in Sardinia.

Revisionism—A modification of Marxism that abandoned Marx's emphasis on revolution and instead called for communist political power based on democratic principles.

Scientific Socialism—Or Marxism, was a philosophy of protest and revolution that advanced the goal of a classless society.

Utopian Socialism—Proposed an equitable solution to improve the distribution of society's wealth; endorsed the productive capacity of industrialism but denounced capitalist-based management.

World History: World War I and Europe in Crisis

April Theses—Lenin's statement of principles in April 1917; it called for the end to the war and advanced a communist domestic agenda for Russia.

Bloc National—French coalition headed by Alexandre Millerand in 1919.

Constituent Assembly—The political body that resulted from the free elections sponsored by Lenin in November 1917; it rejected Bolshevik proposals and when it convened, it was dissolved by communist forces.

Easter Rising—Violent Irish insurrection against British authority in 1916; resulted in enhancing the role of Sinn Fein.

Entente-Cordiale—A colonial settlement between France and England in 1904 that resolved differences in Africa and resulted in a diplomatic *rapprochement*.

July Days—A failed Bolshevik attempt to force the collapse of the Provisional Government in July 1917.

Kronstadt Rebellion—A Soviet naval rebellion in 1921 that resulted from the disastrous economic and social problems that characterized Soviet society.

NEP [New Economic Policy]—Lenin's retreat from communism in 1921 that permitted private property and limited capitalist development.

Provisional Government—Ruled Russia from March through November 1917; it was overthrown by the Bolsheviks.

World History: World War II to the Collapse of the Soviet Union

Appeasement—Policy advanced by Neville Chamberlain during the 1930s that was based on the premise that it was necessary to "correct" the abuses and errors of the Versailles Treaty.

Atlantic Charter—Agreement between Churchill and Roosevelt in August 1941 about war aims and the characteristics of a "new world order."

"Big Three"—Winston Churchill of Great Britain, Franklin Roosevelt of the United States, and Joseph Stalin of the Soviet Union.

Brezhnev Doctrine—Soviet policy that justified armed intervention in suppressing the "liberal" regime of Alexander Dubcek in Czechoslovakia in 1968.

Common Market—The basis for the European Union movement at the close of the twentieth century; initiated with the Schuman Plan in 1951.

Manhattan Project—The American effort to research, develop, and manufacture the atomic bomb.

Marshall Plan—The American European Recovery Program began in 1948 and was designed to assist in the recovery of Western Europe and prevent the further expansion of Soviet influence.

NATO—The North Atlantic Treaty Organization, which was established to defend the west against Soviet aggression.

"Phony War"—War on the Western Front from September 1939 to May 10, 1940, when the Germans launched their offensive against France; it was characterized by a lack of action.

Solidarity Movement—Trade union movement headed by Lech Walesa that forced reform in Communist Poland during the 1980s.

Stalinism—Hard-line rule in Soviet Union and its satellites characterized by an absence of individual freedoms and brutality to preserve order.

Troika—Georgy Malenkov, Lavrenti Beria, and Vyacheslav Molotov shared power in the Soviet Union during the immediate period after Stalin's death in March 1953.

United States History Terms

U.S. History: 1500–1763

Chattel Slaves—Slaves whose status was life-long and would be passed on to their children.

Conquistadores—Independent Spanish adventurers, instrumental in the exploration of the New World.

Creoles—Those of Spanish parentage born in the New World.

Encomiendas—Large manors or estates given as rewards to Spanish *conquistadores*, with Indian slaves ruthlessly managed for their benefit.

Hacienda—An estate similar to the *encomiendas,* but somewhat milder.

Huguenots—French Protestants.

Indentured Servant—A person whose passage to the New World was paid for by an American planter or company in exchange for several years of labor.

Isthmus—A narrow strip of land connecting two larger land masses, with water on two sides.

Joint-Stock Company—A company that raises capital by the sale of shares of stock.

Mayflower Compact—A contract drawn up on board the *Mayflower* to lay the basis for governing Plymouth Colony.

Mercantilism—An economic system based on the belief that the world wealth was finite, and therefore where each nation strove to export more than it imported in order to receive gold and silver, which would make the nation strong both militarily and economically.

Monarch—A ruler, such as a king or a queen, who serves as head of state, and whose term of office is for life.

Northwest Passage—A water route to the Orient through or around the North American continent.

Old Lights/New Lights—Old Lights rejected the religious enthusiasm of the Great Awakening; New Lights accepted it.

Patroon—A large landholder in New Netherlands (present-day New York) who had at least 50 tenant farmers working on his land.

Peninsulares—Natives of Spain in the New World.

Pennsylvania Dutch—Germans who settled in Pennsylvania.

Proprietary Colony—A colony that was owned by an individual, rather than a company.

Puritans—Calvinists who hoped to reform the Church of England.

Separatists—English Protestants who did not believe the Church of England could be saved.

U.S. History: 1763–1787

Boycott—Merchant's refusal to import British goods.

Continentals—Regular soldiers paid by the Continental Congress.

Declaratory Act—An act that, while following the repeal of the Stamp Act, proclaimed the right of Parliament to tax or make laws for the American colonies.

The Enlightenment—An eighteenth-century intellectual movement that emphasized rationalism and human reason as adequate to solve humankind's problems.

Hessians—German mercenaries hired by the British to fight in the American Revolution.

Intolerable Acts—The Coercive Acts were laws passed by Britain to respond to the Boston Tea Party and other acts of American rebellion. The Quebec Act declared Roman Catholicism the official religion of Quebec. These two sets of acts together were called the Intolerable Acts by the American colonists.

Loyalists—American colonists who sided with the British in the American Revolution.

Militia—Citizen-soldiers.

Privateers—Privately owned vessels outfitted with guns and authorized by a warring government to capture enemy merchant ships for profit.

Quartering Act—A law requiring American colonists to provide housing for British troops.

Stamp Act—A direct tax on the American colonies that required stamps to be purchased on everything from newspapers to legal documents.

Sugar Act—A tax on goods imported into the Americas. (Also known as the Revenue Act.)

Tea Act—An act providing for the direct importation of taxed tea from India to America.

Townshend Acts—A program of taxes on the American colonies on imported goods.

Unicameral Legislature—A legislature with one body.

Writs of Assistance—General search warrants issued to help officers stop evasion of Britain's mercantilist trade restrictions.

U.S. History: 1787–1789

Bill of Rights—The first ten amendments to the Constitution, limiting the power of the federal government.

Federalists—Those favoring ratification of the Constitution.

Great Compromise—A plan for the U.S. Constitution that called for a presidency, a Senate with all states represented equally, and a House of Representatives with representation according to population.

New Jersey Plan—A plan for the U.S. Constitution that called for a unicameral legislature with equal representation of the states and sharply increased powers for the national government.

Virginia Plan—A plan for the U.S. Constitution that called for an executive branch and two houses of Congress, each based on population.

U.S. History: 1789–1824

Broad Interpretation—An interpretation of the Constitution as having vested extensive powers in the federal government.

Cabinet—Officials who serve as advisors to the President as well as run the executive department.

Corporation—A business organization used to raise capital and ensure limited liability for its participants.

Cotton Gin—A device used to quickly separate the seeds from the fibers of the cotton plant.

Faction—A group of individuals with shared interests, not taking into account the interests of the society at large.

Mandate—An overwhelming election victory that gives the winner political credit.

Monroe Doctrine—Monroe's statement that European powers could not interfere in the affairs of the American hemisphere.

Nullify—To declare federal law void within a state.

Quids—Republican opponents of Jefferson who accused him of complicity in the Yazoo controversy.

Strict Interpretation—An interpretation of the Constitution holding that any action not specifically permitted was thereby prohibited.

Turnpike—A privately owned toll road.

U.S. History: 1824–1850

Abolitionism—A movement opposed to slavery.

American System—The platform of Henry Clay, providing a high tariff on imports to finance internal improvements.

Kitchen Cabinet—Andrew Jackson's unofficial advisors.

Labor Union—A worker group that fights for better wages and working conditions.

Manifest Destiny—The belief that the American nation was destined to expand all the way to the Pacific Ocean, and possibly embrace Canada to the north and Mexico to the south.

Mountain Men—Men who trapped beavers for their pelts in the Rocky Mountains.

Peculiar Institution—The Southern term for slavery.

Romanticism—An intellectual movement that held a belief in the innate goodness of man, thus in his improvability. It emphasizes emotions and feelings over rationality.

Social Gospel—A religious movement that offered universal salvation.

Spoils System—Giving jobs and other benefits to one's partisan supporters.

Temperance—Opposition to consumption of alcoholic beverages.

Transcendentalism—An intellectual movement that sought to transcend the bounds of the intellect, to strive for emotional understanding, and to attain unity with God, without the help of organized religion.

Underground Railroad—A way that slaves, with the assistance of sympathizers, could escape plantations in the South for the North.

Utopia—A small, cooperative community designed to improve life by rejecting impersonal industrialism.

Yeoman Farmer—A small, independent farmer in the antebellum South.

U.S. History: 1850–1861

Fireeaters—Southern delegates to the Democratic party convention who walked out in protest of the convention's refusal to include a platform plan demanding federal protection of slavery in all the territories.

Forty-Niners—Gold seekers from the eastern U.S. who went to California.

Free-Soil Party—A political party that stood for prohibiting slavery from newly acquired territories.

Nativists—Americans who were alarmed about increasing immigration from Germany and Ireland.

Popular Sovereignty—A process where the residents of a territory would decide whether slavery was to be permitted when the territory became a state.

Young America—An aggressive program of economic and territorial expansion.

U.S. History: 1861–1877

Anaconda Plan—The Northern strategy for the Civil War. It included a naval blockade to shut out supplies from Europe, a campaign to take the Mississippi River, and the taking of a few strategic points and waiting for pro-Union sentiment in the South to overthrow the secessionists.

Carpetbaggers—Northerners who came to the South to participate in Reconstruction governments.

Copperheads—Northerners who opposed the war.

Crime of '73—What pro-inflation forces called the demonetization of silver.

Greenbacks—An unbacked fiat currency issued by the Union to help fund the Civil War.

Ironclad Oath—An oath required by Radical Republicans, that a requisite number of Southerners would have to take before the state could be readmitted to the Union. It states that the Southerner was now loyal and had never been disloyal to the Union.

Ironclad Ship—A technological innovation during the Civil War, in which a ship was protected from cannon fire by iron plates bolted onto the wooden sides.

Laissez-faire—The belief that government should not interfere in the economy.

Pocket Veto—Preventing a bill from becoming law by letting the bill expire without signing it.

Reconstruction—The process by which the defeated Southern states would be admitted back into the Union.

Redemption—The end of Reconstruction governments.

Scalawags—Southerners who supported Reconstruction programs.

U.S. History: 1877–1912

Big Stick Diplomacy—Using American military power to fortify the diplomatic policies of the United States.

Boxers—Chinese nationalists who fought against foreign interests in China.

Bull Moose Party—Another name for the Progressive party.

Dollar Diplomacy—Using American economic power to fortify the diplomatic policies of the United States.

Gilded Age—The period between the 1870s and 1890s when the United States emerged as the world's leading industrial and agricultural producer.

Half-Breeds—The Republican faction that pushed for civil service reform and merit appointments to government posts.

Muckrakers—Investigative journalists and authors who exposed corruption in business and government.

Mugwumps—Independent Republicans who favored civil service reforms.

New Imperialism—Expansion that replaced territorial colonialism with finding markets for surplus industrial production, access to raw materials, and opportunities for overseas investment during domestic economic depression.

Open Door Policy—Declared that trade with China should be open to all nations.

Populist—A political coalition of agrarians with urban workers and the middle class. Its goals included monetization of silver, a graduated income tax, public ownership of railroads, telegraph, and telephone systems, an eight-hour day, and a ban on private armies used to break up strikes.

Progressivism—A political movement calling for rejuvenation of free enterprise capitalism and the destruction of illegal monopolies. It also called for civil service reform and honest and efficient government.

Reservation—Isolated lands where Native Americans were compelled to live.

Social Darwinism—An application of Darwin's theory of evolution, survival of the fittest, to justify unequal distribution of wealth by claiming that God granted wealth to the fittest.

Stalwarts—The Republican faction that favored the spoils system of political patronage.

Yellow Journalism—Sensationalist newspapers that encouraged direct military intervention on behalf of Cuban independence.

U.S. History: 1912–1920

Arabic Pledge—The German pledge to stop submarine attacks on unarmed passenger vessels.

League of Nations—An international orga- nization to promote peaceful resolution of international conflicts. It called on all members to protect the territorial integrity and the political independence of all other members.

Liberty Bonds—Bonds sold to the American public to fund the federal wartime debt.

Prohibition—A Constitutional amendment that prohibited the sale and manufacture of alcoholic beverages in the United States.

Sussex Pledge—The German pledge to cease submarine attacks on all shipping.

U.S. History: 1920–1929

Big Ticket Items—Large, expensive consumer items such as automobiles, refrigerators, and furniture.

Black Tuesday—October 29, 1929, the stock market fell about 40 points with 16.5 mil- lion shares traded.

Creationism—Belief in the biblical account of the origin of the universe and life on earth.

Flappers—Young women who were indepen- dent, assertive, and promiscuous.

Installment Credit—Purchasing expensive goods by making monthly payments.

Lost Generation—Young writers of the 1920s who were dissatisfied with the hypocrisy and materialism of contemporary Ameri- can society.

Oligopoly—A situation in which three or four firms dominate an industry.

Open Shop—A nonunion workplace.

Standard Metropolitan Area—An area with a central city of at least 50,000 in popula- tion.

Welfare Capitalism—A system where a firm provides job satisfaction so workers would not see the need for a union.

U.S. History: 1929–1941

Economic Royalists—Business people Roos- evelt charged with seeking only their own power and wealth by opposing the New Deal.

Hoovervilles—Empty spaces around cities where the homeless would set up make- shift shacks to live in.

Hundred Days—The period immediately following Roosevelt's first inauguration during which Congress passed the most important legislation of the New Deal.

Isolationism—The belief that the United States should stay out of foreign wars and prob- lems.

Margin Trading—Purchasing stock by borrow- ing 90 percent of the purchase through a broker's loan, and putting up the stock as collateral.

New Deal—Roosevelt's plan for coping with the Depression. It included social programs as well as regulations on busi- nesses.

Underconsumption—An economic situation that occurs when ordinary farmers and workers do not have money to continue purchasing products.

U.S. History: 1941–1960

Alienation—The condition of being isolated or separated from mainstream society.

Big Three—The leaders of the major Allied powers: Roosevelt, Churchill, and Stalin.

Containment—A strategy that called for containing communism and preventing it from spreading further.

Dixiecrats—Southern Democrats who opposed Truman due to his support of civil rights. They nominated Strom Thurmond as their presidential candidate in 1948.

Manhattan Project—The project to design and construct a portable atomic bomb.

Marshall Plan—The European Recovery Program providing more than $12 billion in aid to rebuild Europe.

NATO—The North Atlantic Treaty Organization, which pledged that an attack against one member was an attack against all.

Truman Doctrine—President Truman stated that the United States must support free peoples who were resisting communist domination.

White Flight—The migration of whites from cities to suburbs as blacks migrated to northern cities.

U.S. History: 1960–1972

Counterculture—Young people alienated by bureaucracy, materialism, and the Vietnam War, who attempted to create alternative societies.

Détente—A French term that meant a relaxation in tensions between two governments.

Domino Theory—A justification for American involvement in Vietnam, claiming that if Vietnam fell to the communists, all of Southeast Asia would fall.

Doves—Those who favored withdrawal from the Vietnam War.

Great Society—Lyndon Johnson's program of social reform, including federal assistance in housing, education, and health.

Hawks—Those who favored continued involvement in the Vietnam War.

Hippies—Young people who experimented with Eastern religions, recreational drugs, and sex.

New Left—Young radicals of the 1960s who centered their political activities in and around college and university campuses. Strategies often involved protests, demonstrations, and sit-ins.

Vietcong—The pro-Communist Vietnamese forces.

Vietnamization—The effort to build up South Vietnamese troops while withdrawing American troops.

U.S. History: 1972–Present

AIDS—Acquired Immune Deficiency Syndrome, a disease that weakens and destroys the immune system, primarily spread through sexual contact and using contaminated needles.

Contras—Right wing guerrillas who fought the leftist Sandinista government of Nicaragua.

Junk Bonds—High interest bonds with a low investment grade.

Moral Majority—Christian Conservatives, led by Reverend Jerry Falwell, who favored prayer and teaching of creationism in public schools, opposed abortion, pornography, ERA, and supported a strong national defense.

Pro-Choice—Those who wish to keep abortion legal.

Pro-Life—Those who wish to make abortion illegal.

Strategic Defense Initiative—A defense system, using satellites to prevent enemy missiles from striking the United States.

Superfund—A dedicated federal fund for toxic waste site cleanups.

Supply-Side Economics—An economic theory that claims that if government policies leave more money in the hands of people, then they will invest it and stimulate the economy.

Underclass—A class characterized by extreme poverty and geographic isolation, often in inner-cities.

Your Test-Day Checklist

☐ Get a good night's sleep. Tired test-takers consistently perform poorly.

☐ Wake up early.

☐ Dress comfortably. Keep your clothing temperature appropriate. You'll be sitting in yout test clothes for hours. Clothes that are itchy, tight, too warm, or too cold take away from your comfort level.

☐ Eat a good breakfast.

☐ Take these with you to the test center:
- Several sharpened No. 2 pencils. Pencils are not provided at the test center.
- A ballpoint pen
- Admission ticket
- Two forms of ID. One must be a current, government-issued identification bearing your photograph and signature.

☐ Arrive at the test center early. Remember, many test centers do not allow you into a test session after the test has begun.

☐ Compose your thoughts and try to relax before the test.

Remember that eating, drinking, and smoking are prohibited. Calculators, dictionaries, textbooks, notebooks, briefcases, and packages are also prohibited.